Edition 1.2 – 2024

Copyright © 2021 The Mindfulness Initiative
Sheffield, S1, United Kingdom
Registered charity number 1179834 (England & Wales)

ISBN 978-1-913353-04-9

Implementation Guide Team
Research & Writing: Katherine Weare and Adrian Bethune
Updated by Katherine Weare, February 2024
Editing: Jamie Bristow, Ruth Ormston
Design: J-P Stanway

This work is licensed under the Creative Commons Attribution, NonCommercial, No derivatives 4.0 International license (CC BY-NC-ND 4.0). The full text of this license is available here.

(i) **Attribution** – You must give appropriate credit, provide a link to the license, and indicate if changes were made. You may do so in any reasonable manner, but not in any way that suggests the licensor endorses you or your use.

($) **NonCommercial** – You may not use this material for commercial purposes.

(=) **NoDerivatives** – If you remix, transform, or build upon the material, you may not distribute the modified material.

About The Mindfulness Initiative

The Mindfulness Initiative grew out of a programme of mindfulness teaching for politicians in the UK Parliament. We work with legislators around the world who practise mindfulness and help them to make capacities of heart and mind serious considerations of public policy. We investigate the benefits, limitations, opportunities and challenges in accessing and implementing mindfulness training and educate leaders, service-commissioners and the general public based on these findings.

www.themindfulnessinitiative.org/

Please support our work

The Mindfulness Initiative doesn't receive any public funding and in order to retain its neutral and trusted advisory position in the sector cannot generate revenue from competitive products or services. As such, we are entirely dependent on charitable gifts to sustain our work. If you find this implementation guide helpful, please consider making a contribution. Visit www.themindfulnessinitiative.org/appeal/donate to make a one-time or recurring donation.

Endorsements

> **Deep bow of appreciation to the entire team for the incredible (also elegant and balanced) work of the Mindfulness Initiative.**

Jon Kabat-Zinn

> **An incredibly useful piece of work – as you would expect from the team at The Mindfulness Initiative. It is authoritative, clear, comprehensive and really practical. It will guide the development of mindfulness in education for years to come.**

@GuyClaxton – Honorary Professor of Education, University of Bristol; Visiting Professor, King's College London; Emeritus Professor, University of Winchester

> **One of the greatest challenges of humanity is for us to understand our own minds. So much suffering to self and others is caused partly by lack of insight into what drives us. This wonderful initiative to bring the wisdom of mindfulness to our children could not come too soon.**

Professor Paul Gilbert. PhD, FBPsS, OBE

> **A comprehensive, accessible and inspiring 'must read' guide for all schools on a mindfulness journey.**

Amanda Bailey – Executive Director: Finance and Operations Star Academies

> **The Guide is a superb resource for anyone interested in implementing mindfulness in schools. Practical and evidence-based, we are recommending this as an excellent place to start.**

Chivonne Preston – CEO, The Mindfulness in Schools Project

About the authors

Professor Katherine Weare

Katherine Weare is Emeritus Professor at the University of Southampton and co-lead for Education for the Mindfulness Initiative. Starting out as a secondary school teacher, Katherine is known internationally for her ground-breaking work on mindfulness in education. This grows out of a long career focusing on research and development on well-being, mental health, and social and emotional learning in education.

Katherine has published some of the most influential books, papers and reviews in the field, advised UK governments, the European Union and the World Health Organisation, and led on the development of practical strategies and programmes across most European countries which have been sustained to this day. These include the seminal 'Social and Emotional Aspects of Learning' (SEAL) programme across the UK, and the 'European Network of Healthy Schools' across Europe, both of which put wellbeing at the heart of the whole school process. Her recent book, co-written with Zen Master Thich Nhat Hanh 'Happy Teachers Change The World: A Guide to Cultivating Mindfulness in Education' has been translated into 7 languages and won several awards. She is currently leading the development of the vibrant 'Community of Contemplative Education' for Mind and Life Europe.

Adrian Bethune

Adrian Bethune is a part-time school teacher and wellbeing-lead governor at a primary school in Buckinghamshire, the Education Policy co-lead at the Mindfulness Initiative and founder of Teachappy. In 2012, he was awarded a 'Happy Hero' medal by Lord Richard Layard at the House of Lords for his work on developing wellbeing in schools. In 2015, he was invited to speak at the Action For Happiness event, Creating A Happier World, on stage with the Dalai Lama.

Adrian is author of the award-winning Wellbeing In The Primary Classroom – A Practical Guide To Teaching Happiness (Bloomsbury, 2018) and co-author with Dr Emma Kell of A Little Guide to Teacher Wellbeing and Self-care (Sage, 2020). He speaks and trains internationally, writes regularly for the Times Education Supplement and has contributed to several other books including Global Perspectives in Positive Education (John Catt, 2018), Children and Young People's Mental Health Today (Pavilion, 2019), and Just Great Teaching (Bloomsbury, 2019). He is also lead author and designer of the Oxford University Press International Curriculum for Wellbeing.

Acknowledgments

Grateful thanks to the funders of the Mindfulness Initiative for all their faith and support in the work that we do. Thank you to the Lostand Foundation, Mindful Trust and Sankalpa.

We consulted an expert steering group in detail about this document and its inception, as well as various other advisors whose wisdom we drew upon. All were extremely generous in providing their time, expertise and feedback, and we have huge appreciation for their contributions, advice and support.

With particular thanks to:

Amanda Bailey, Star Academies
Caroline Barratt, Contemplative Pedagogy, University of Essex
Michael Bready, Youth Mindfulness
Vidyamala Burch, Breathworks
Richard Burnett, Mindfulness in Schools Project (MISP)
Guy Claxton, Professor, University of Winchester
Dusana Dorjee, University of York
Clare Eddison, Headteacher, Dharma School, Brighton.
Claire Kelly, MISP
Richard Layard, Professor, Action for Happiness, London School of Economics
Jan Lever, Jigsaw
Liz Lord, School Liaison, MYRIAD Project, Oxford Mindfulness Centre
Frances Maratos, Compassion in Schools
Cathie Paine, Deputy CEO, Reach 2, Academy for Leadership
Chivonne Preston, MISP
David Rycroft, Mind with Heart
Julia Organ, MindUp
Sarah Silverton, The Present
Orlaith O'Sullivan, Wake Up Schools
Liz Williams, Policy Lead Welsh Government

Mark Williamson, Director, Action for Happiness

We are also very grateful to the schools and teachers who provided us with invaluable case studies to really show the theory we write about being put into practice:

Andrew Thomas, Cathedral School Cardiff
Burgh Primary School, Rutherglen, South Lanarkshire
Culross Primary, Fife
Dacorum Education Support centre, Hertfordshire
Eyres Monsell Primary School, Leicester
Lynburn Primary School, Dunfermline, Fife
The Reach2 Academy, Burton upon Trent
Sarah Hegarty Abertillery Learning Community Secondary Campus, Blaenau, Gwent
Springboard College, Letchworth
West Rise Community Infant School, Eastbourne, East Sussex

and to the following internal and external teachers who brought the case studies to our attention:

Liz Cain, With Peace In Mind
Karen Cronin
Vicky McCool, headteacher, Burgh Primary School South Lanarkshire
Jen La Trobe, Intriguing Young Minds
Lynne Weir, headteacher, West Rise Community Infant School, Eastbourne, East Sussex
Claire Winter, Dacorum Education Support Centre, Hertfordshire

Foreword

The demands we put on children and educators to be the best that they can be in a rapidly changing world have perhaps never been greater, whilst a seemingly inexorable rise in digital distractions undermines focused learning. We have long told children to 'pay attention'; now more than ever we must teach them how. The regulation of attention, along with the development of other cognitive, social and emotional resources vital for the 21st century, must find their place alongside more traditional learning.

Similarly, we have long known that the majority of mental health problems start in childhood, and that prevention and early intervention could have dramatic, life-long implications for success and happiness. Whilst much progress has been made in schools to address this, it's clear that new innovations and greater investment are still required.

As a former Children's Minister and current Co-Chair of the All-Party Parliamentary Group on Mindfulness, these are a few reasons that I am particularly enthusiastic about the prospect of wider access to mindfulness teaching in British schools. Education was one of four areas that our cross-party group, with support from The Mindfulness Initiative, examined in the first public policy review of mindfulness-based interventions, culminating in the publication of the Mindful Nation UK report in 2015. We heard evidence from scientists, teachers and pupils with education providing some of the most compelling personal testimony from the 12-month enquiry.

Our report concluded that, based on what was then around 50 peer-reviewed studies, mindfulness was starting to impact on some key policy challenges for children and young people, particularly academic attainment, mental health, wellbeing, social and emotional learning (including resilience and character) and behaviour. It commented that the research was still young, and most of the studies had a small sample size. We detected a growing consensus that three features are particularly important to effectiveness and sustainability: the quality and experience of the teacher's own mindfulness practice; how a programme is implemented; and the use of a whole school approach.

As this new evidence-based guide shows, the core thinking, evidence reviews and conclusions of the Mindful Nation UK report still basically hold true almost six years on, and the field of mindfulness in education, in both the UK and internationally, has developed steadily rather than undergoing any seismic shifts. The evidence base for the outcomes of mindfulness has slowly increased in size and robustness, and the programmes that were present in the UK in 2015 continue to develop steadily, with a few more coming into existence. The largest and most comprehensive study of mindfulness in schools, a collaboration between the Universities of Oxford, Cambridge and UCL, will start reporting its results later this year. I hope that this will further add to the already compelling case for widespread implementation.

In this context, I warmly congratulate the Education Policy Co-Leads at The Mindfulness Initiative, Professor Katherine Weare and Adrian Bethune, for pulling together this comprehensive, timely and much-needed implementation guide for educators. It will undoubtedly prove to be an invaluable resource for many years to come and will hopefully facilitate schools in improving many thousands of young lives.

Tim Loughton MP
Co-Chair of the All-Party Parliamentary Group on Mindfulness

February 2021

Contents

How to use this guide

About this guide 13

How you might use this guide 13

What is in each chapter? 14

PART ONE
UNDERSTANDING MINDFULNESS

CHAPTER 1
What is mindfulness?

Summary of Chapter 1 18

What do we mean by 'mindfulness'? 19

What makes a course 'mindfulness'? 20

Essential features of any mindfulness course
(the warp) 20

An antidote to wandering and distracted
mind states 20

Mindfulness helps us recognise and
embrace possibilities 20

A new relationship with the mind – in the body and
in the world 21

Stepping back from thoughts 21

More than calmness and relaxation – it's cultivating
a new relationship to our experience 21

Core values: cultivating compassion, kindness
and a social ethic 22

A human capacity that underlies our happiness 23

Mindfulness practice can be the antidote to
the modern condition 23

Preserving the natural mindfulness of childhood? 23

Some further myths and misconceptions
about mindfulness 24

PART TWO
DOES MINDFULNESS WORK – AND IF SO, HOW?

CHAPTER 2:
The outcomes of mindfulness: a summary

Summary of Chapter 2 28

What – in summary – does the evidence show? 29

    Mindfulness is foundational 29

    Mindfulness shows a wide range of positive outcomes for teachers 29

    Mindfulness shows a wide range of positive outcomes for children and young people in school contexts 29

    Other significant findings 30

    How to read the evidence 30

CHAPTER 3:
The outcomes of mindfulness for teachers

Summary of Chapter 3 32

Wellbeing 33

    What is 'wellbeing' in research terms? 33

    Can wellbeing be measured? 33

    Teachers' wellbeing 33

    Impacts on teachers' physical health and wellbeing 33

    Self-compassion 34

    Mindfulness helps address mental health problems in teachers 34

Mindfulness and teacher effectiveness 35

    Emotion regulation 35

    Changing relationship to experience 35

Responding more effectively to student behaviour 36

Creating effective and connected classroom climates 36

CHAPTER 4:
The outcomes of mindfulness for children and young people

Summary of Chapter 4 37

The wellbeing of children and young people in schools 38

    The impact of mindfulness on student wellbeing 38

    Mindfulness helps address mental health problems in young people 39

Cultivating social and emotional skills 40

Mindfulness and compassion 41

Impacts on cognition, learning and attainment 41

Impacts on academic performance 42

Impacts on behaviour 42

Unexpected findings from a large scale RCT point to the need to scale up carefully 43

CONTENTS

CHAPTER 5:
How mindfulness works – the mechanisms and the neuroscience

Summary of Chapter 5...44

Why do the psychology and the neuroscience of mindfulness matter?..45

The cheering news for educators about neuroplasticity 45

Mindfulness creates changes in the brain 45

    It's complex 46

Four key mechanisms that mindfulness develops, and the neuroscience that underpins them 46

Attention 46

    Why does the attention matter to education? 46

    What is the edidence for the impact of mindfulness on attention? 47

    How does mindfulness impact on the parts of the brain particularly involved in the attention 47

Metacognition: Standing back from the thought process 47

    Why does metacognition matter to education......... 47

What is the evidence for the impact of mindfulness on metacognition? 48

How does mindfulness impact on the parts of the brain particularly involved in metacognition..48

Emotion regulation..48

    Why does emotion regulation matter in education?...48

    What is the evidence of the impact of mindfulness on emotion regulation? 48

    How does mindfulness impact on the parts of the brain particularly involved with emotion regulation? 49

Self-regulation: the master competence..........................49

    Why does self-regulation matter to education?.......49

    What is the evidence for the impact of mindfulness on self-regulation? 49

    How does mindfulness impact on the parts of the brain particularly involved in self-regulation? 49

PART THREE
IMPLEMENTING MINDFULNESS IN SCHOOLS

CHAPTER 6
Establishing the foundations

Summary of Chapter 6 54

Integrating mindfulness with educational language and thinking 55

Matching mindfulness to the school's priorities and needs 55

Establishing effective champions 56

Engaging the Senior Leadership Team (SLT) 56

Spreading understanding across the school community 57

Using inspirational first-hand experience and testimonials 58

Allocating sufficient resources 58

CHAPTER 7
Developing mindfulness for teachers

Summary of Chapter 7 59

Why do we need to start with the teachers? 60

    Ensuring teachers work with a full model of mindfulness 60

Routes into training to teach mindfulness 61

    Undertaking an eight-week course 61

    Foundation courses run by programmes 61

    Face to face or online? 62

Teachers and students learn together 62

    The need for more data 62

Giving ongoing support 63

Supportive networks of schools 63

CHAPTER 8
Teaching mindfulness to students

Summary of Chapter 8 64

Choosing the approach 65

    The teacher creates their own approach 65

    Choosing an established programme: exploring fit and feasibility 65

    Programme fidelity or adaptation? 65

    Using an internal or external teacher of mindfulness? 66

Moving into the classroom 67

    Mindfulness teaching is founded on relationships 67

    Engaging teaching and learning methods 67

    The central role of reflective enquiry 68

    Encouraging practice outside class 69

    Using peer learning 70

Taking care of students and their vulnerabilities 72

Fitting mindfulness to the needs of students 72

CHAPTER 9
Embedding and sustaining mindfulness within a whole school approach

Summary of Chapter 9 73

What is meant by a whole school approach? 74

    In mental health and wellbeing 74

    In social and emotional learning 74

    How does mindfulness relate to SEL? 75

CONTENTS

  Within work on key values: compassion,
  gratitude and connection 76

  Mindfulness and nature 76

  With neuroscience education 77

  Within the process of learning 77

Involving parents and the wider community 78

Embedding and sustaining in the classroom
and school climate, culture and ethos 79

A congruent working environment 79

CHAPTER 10
Evaluating mindfulness in a school

Summary of Chapter 10 81

Before starting – questions for initial reflection 82

Evaluating acceptability 82

Evaluation as a process – action research 83

The value of both quantitative and
qualitative data 84

Quantitative methods and designs 84

  Before and after 84

  Control trials/randomised control trials (RCTs) 84

Qualitative methods and designs 85

Online resources 86

Some further sources of support 87

  On evaluating mindfulness 87

  On evaluating wellbeing 87

  On the research process 87

POST-SCRIPT

The immediate priorities: embedding in
school contexts 88

Mindfulness has a core role in helping education
respond to 21st century challenges 89

What mindfulness contributes to educational and
social transformation 90

APPENDICES

APPENDIX 1:
Table of mindfulness programmes
in the UK 91

APPENDIX 2:
Systematic reviews and meta-analyses of
teachers and school aged youth 96

APPENDIX 3:
Outcome measures often used in evaluating
the impact of Mindfulness-Based Interventions
in school contexts 99

  Mindfulness 99

  Psycho-social outcomes 100

  Social and emotional learning 101

  School climate 101

  Physiological measures 102

APPENDIX 4:
Useful websites and apps 103

APPENDIX 5:
Core reading 105

APPENDIX 6:
References and notes 108

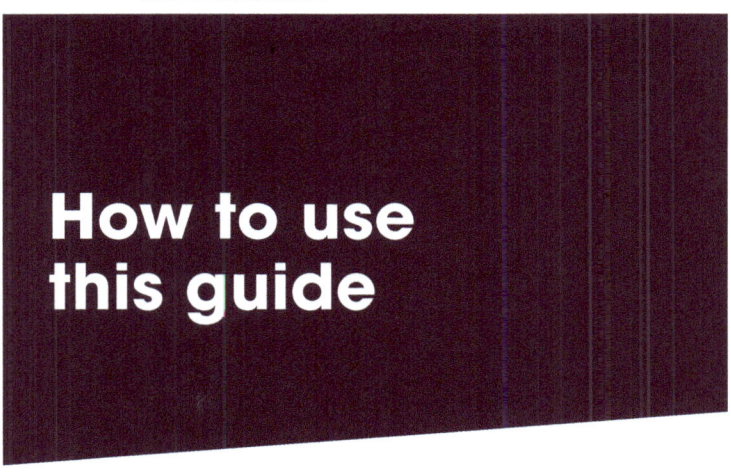

How to use this guide

About this guide

This guide aims to provide practical, trustworthy and evidence-based guidance on developing mindfulness in schools and in the whole community who work and learn there. It attempts to bring some clarity to an area of education that is growing fast, and with very promising evidence and much enthusiasm from schools, but which can be confusing and is often riddled with misunderstandings.

The guidance is based on:

- international scientific evidence of the outcomes of mindfulness in schools.

- international empirical research on implementing and embedding mindfulness in schools for teachers and students.

- advice from a range of experts, drawn from innovators in schools, programme developers, researchers and academics and contemplative practitioners.

The guidance is for a range of audiences:

- those who are actively working in the 3-18 UK education systems initiating, leading and developing practical work on in school settings, or policy mindfulness, with children and young people and the adults who work with them. The detail and application of the advice has a specifically UK focus.

- those from other parts of the world who are working in this area, and who should find the principles and the evidence base on outcomes and implementation relevant to their situation.

- those programme makers who are developing and leading mindfulness courses and practices specifically for use in schools or with young people.

- those who are working in related areas such as compassion, mental health, emotional and social education, personal development and reflective learning who want to explore what policy and practice around mindfulness has to offer in the joint effort to make schools more humane and effective places.

- those who are broadly interested in what is happening with mindfulness in schools.

How you might use this guide

We hope you have time to read this guide from cover to cover, but as time is often tight:

- Whatever your particular interest, if you are involved in implementation, creating policy, or you just want an overview, we recommend you read Chapter 1 on understanding mindfulness and the summaries at the start of each chapter so you get a sense of the whole picture.

- If you are mainly interested in the practicalities of implementation, focus on the detail of the chapters in part three (Chapters 6, 7, 8, 9 and 10). You should also find Appendices 4 and 5 useful.

- If you want to understand the evidence, mechanisms and neuroscience, focus on the detail of the chapters in part two (Chapters 2, 3, 4 and 5). You should also find Appendix 2 useful.

- If you want a greater understanding about the issues around evaluating mindfulness in a school setting, including some guidance on the practicalities of how to do this, focus on the detail of Chapter 10. You should also find Appendices 2 and 3 useful.

HOW TO USE THIS GUIDE

What is in each chapter?

PART ONE:
UNDERSTANDING MINDFULNESS

CHAPTER 1 What is mindfulness? This chapter clarifies what we mean by 'mindfulness', its essential features and how it works. It explores the values mindfulness cultivates such as open-mindedness, curiosity, kindness, and compassion, the distinctive features that make a course 'mindfulness;' and some myths and misconceptions.

PART TWO:
DOES MINDFULNESS WORK – AND IF SO, HOW?

CHAPTER 2 Summary and overview of the evidence base: Gives an overview of the evidence for the wide range of outcomes of mindfulness-based interventions for teachers, children and young people; explores the size and quality of the evidence base; and unpacks different types of evidence.

CHAPTER 3 Outcomes for teachers: Explores the outcomes of mindfulness for school staff in more detail, unpacking impacts on psychological and physical wellbeing, tackling mental health difficulties, and teacher effectiveness. It illustrates the discussion with brief case studies.

CHAPTER 4 Outcomes for children and young people: Explores in more detail the outcomes of mindfulness for children and young people, looking at psychological and physical wellbeing, tackling mental health difficulties, cultivating social and emotional skills, cognition, learning and attainment, and behaviour. It illustrates the discussion with brief case studies.

CHAPTER 5 How does mindfulness work? Mechanisms and neuroscience: Explores what psychology and neuroscience say about how mindfulness might 'work' in terms of shaping the brain and underlying psychological constructs. It examines four underlying psycho-physiological mechanism impacted by mindfulness practice, namely attention, metacognition, emotion regulation, and self-regulation, and explores why they matter to education and the areas of the brain to which they relate.

PART THREE:
PUTTING MINDFULNESS INTO PRACTICE IN SCHOOLS

CHAPTER 6 Establishing the foundations: Discusses the importance of some key foundational concepts, including: integrating mindfulness with educational language and thinking; matching the evidence to the school's priorities and needs; establishing effective champions; engaging the Senior Leadership Team; ensuring widespread understanding of mindfulness; using inspirational testimonials; and allocating sufficient resources.

CHAPTER 7 Mindfulness for teachers: Explores why mindfulness in schools starts with developing mindfulness for teachers and other adults, outlines the issues around ensuring good-quality and sufficient training for the adults, and suggests ways to provide ongoing support and staff development.

CHAPTER 8 Mindfulness for school children and young people: Explores the key issues to consider when teaching mindfulness to the young, including: what approach or programme to use, the use of outside or inside facilitators, and programme fidelity or adaption. Once the basics are established, issues that then emerge include the importance of sound relationships, using engaging methods, reflective enquiry, and peer learning, encouraging practice outside class and taking care of students and their vulnerabilities.

CHAPTER 9 Embedding mindfulness in the practices and ethos of the whole school approach: Explores ways in which mindfulness is being embedded within many areas of school life, including work on mental health and wellbeing, social and emotional learning, values, neuroscience, mindfulness and nature, the process of learning, the involvement of parents, and within school and classroom climate and ethos.

CHAPTER 10 Evaluating mindfulness in a school: Aims to demystify and encourage simple evaluation, links process evaluation and action research with school improvement and accountability, explores evaluation using both quantitative and qualitative methods; and clarifies what is meant by before and after; control trials and randomised control trials.

POST-SCRIPT

WHAT'S NEXT? Where the future of mindfulness in education might be heading.

APPENDICES

APPENDIX 1 A table of mindfulness programmes for schools currently running in the UK, outlining their characteristics.

APPENDIX 2 An annotated list of the most recent systematic reviews and meta-analyses of the outcome of mindfulness on teachers and school students.

APPENDIX 3 An annotated list of measures currently often used to evaluate mindfulness and its outcomes with school students and teachers.

APPENDIX 4 An annotated list of useful weblinks and apps.

APPENDIX 5 An annotated reading list of key current literature and resources.

APPENDIX 6 References and notes.

Part One

UNDERSTANDING MINDFULNESS

CHAPTER 1

What is mindfulness?

Summary of Chapter 1

- Mindfulness means intentionally paying attention to present-moment experience, inside ourselves, our minds and bodies, and in our environment, with an attitude of openness, curiosity, kindness and care.

- Mindfulness is a natural human capacity, cultivated by ancient wisdom traditions, that has long been valued as underlying authentic happiness, coping with difficulty, and the ability to live an ethical life.

- In modern times mindfulness practices have been combined with psychological and wellbeing theories and developed into secular teachings. Modern mindfulness has been the subject of many scientific trials and has shown clear and beneficial outcomes for human flourishing.

- Mindfulness is an antidote to wandering and distracted mind states, helping us step back from our thoughts and feelings and freeing us to recognise and embrace all kinds of possibilities.

- A mindfulness course helps participants develop a new relationship with their experience, 'moving towards' their experiences, including difficult ones. It cultivates qualities such as joy, compassion, wisdom, equanimity, the ability to pay attention, relate effectively to the emotions and to engage in more skilful action.

- Mindfulness has to be practised. Courses engage participants in a sustained, intensive training in mindfulness meditation supported by an experiential enquiry-based learning process.

- Mindfulness is not: value free, clearing the mind of thoughts, just calmness and relaxation, inherently religious, a way of keeping children quiet, or an alternative to addressing the structural causes of stress.

What do we mean by 'mindfulness'?

There is much confusion about what the word 'mindfulness' actually means. A clear starting point for a precise and helpful definition derives from the ground-breaking work by the seminal thinker and practitioner Prof. Jon Kabat-Zinn. It is the kind of definition which has widespread acceptance in the mindfulness community.[1]

There are three interrelated core elements to this kind of definition – intention, attention and attitude.

- When we practise being mindful, as best we can right now, we approach whatever is happening in the present moment with a clear intention to focus the attention in a particular way.

- We bring our attention to the present moment and what is happening within or around us, as we are experiencing it in both mind and body.

- We approach this present-moment experience with an attitude of care, acceptance, kindness and friendliness, equanimity, and open-minded, non-judgmental curiosity.

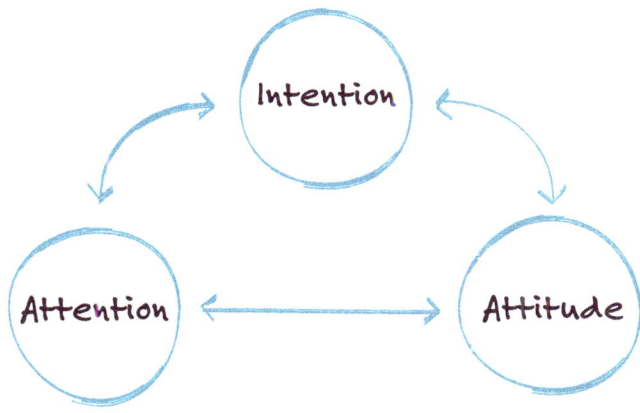

From Shapiro, S., Carlson, L., Astin, J., Freedman, B. (2018) Mechanisms of Mindfulness. Journal of Clinical Psychology www.semanticscholar.org/author/John-A.-Astin/3657288

Teachers sometimes refer to 'the what and the how' of mindfulness - what we are doing when we are mindful (paying attention on purpose) and how we do it (intentionally, with an attitude of open-mindedness, curiosity and care).

> **Mindfulness means intentionally paying attention to present-moment experience, inside ourselves, our minds and bodies, as well as in our environment, with an attitude of openness, curiosity, kindness and care.**
>
> *Kabat-Zinn*

Ancient wisdom supported by modern science

Mindfulness is not a modern invention; it is a human capacity, the value of which has long been apparent through the ages. The cultivation of mindfulness and the qualities that can come from regular formal and informal practice, such as clarity, calm, steadiness, equanimity, open-mindedness, compassion and skilful action, have been a part of many religious and wisdom traditions from both East and West dating back many thousands of years.

In a dramatic shift over the last 40 years, mindfulness practices have been combined with modern psychological and wellbeing theories, and developed into secular teachings that have been the subject of thousands of scientific trials on their impact. There have been increasing efforts to discover and understand the underlying psychological and neurological mechanisms behind the process.

For several decades now, adults have been learning mindfulness through evidence-based '8-week courses' including Mindfulness-Based Stress Reduction (MBSR), originally developed by Jon Kabat-Zinn, or Mindfulness-Based Cognitive Therapy (MBCT) developed in the UK from the MBSR template, which focusses particularly on tackling depression. They have been taught to general and clinical populations of adults, and with an increasingly strong research base, including many randomised control trials (RCTs). Nowadays these courses, and closely related ones, are also being taught online and through books and apps.

WHAT IS MINDFULNESS?

What makes a course 'mindfulness'?

Mindfulness has now spread into many new areas, including education. A seminal paper 'What defines mindfulness-based programs? The warp and the weft' written by those at the heart of the international field[2] outlined the essential features (the 'warp') of any intervention that can properly be termed 'mindfulness', while allowing for contextual adaptations in different settings such as schools (the 'weft').

Essential features of any mindfulness course (the warp)

- It aims to help participants develop a new relationship with their experience, with a focus on the present moment and 'moving towards' experience.

- It aims to cultivate qualities such as joy, compassion, wisdom, equanimity and greater attentional, emotional and behavioural self-regulation.

- It engages participants in a sustained intensive training in mindfulness meditation practice.

- It engages participants in an experiential enquiry-based learning process and in exercises to develop understanding.

An antidote to wandering and distracted mind states

Mindfulness is often presented as a contrast to mindlessness - the 'automatic pilot' of unawareness in which we can live too much of our lives, caught up in the thought stream, away in the past and the future. This automatic pattern of thinking can often be accompanied by negative rumination or anxiety. Our minds tend to jump to unnecessary and self-limiting judgments built on well-rehearsed mindsets. Nowadays we are often ripe for distraction by our electronic devices and the news feed.

A landmark study at Harvard University used phone-tracking technology and found that participants spent nearly half of their time in a state of mindless mind wandering, and that this left people less satisfied with their lives. They suggest, 'a human mind is a wandering mind, and a wandering mind is an unhappy mind'.[3]

> **Mindfulness lets our brains cool down so they can bubble up with ideas.**
>
> *Pupil, aged 9*

Mindfulness helps us recognise and embrace possibilities

Mindfulness is about freedom, not restriction, and is not the enemy of feeling or thought, or indeed of daydreaming, playfulness and occasional mind wandering. All of these are vital processes underlying the human capacity to live fully and make sense of the world - to innovate, problem solve, relate effectively to others, create and fully experience life. Mindfulness can help us get in touch with a greater range of capacities and possibilities through relating to our experience in new ways.

- The practice of mindfulness intends to cultivate greater choice and control over our mind and body states, noticing where and how we place our attention, noticing without judgment where the mind has gone and moving it more flexibly and intentionally in directions we prefer to enable us to act more effectively when we choose.

- A simple definition of mindfulness is 'knowing what you are doing when you are doing it'.

WHAT IS MINDFULNESS?

Recognising the role of the attention in education is not a new fad. The foundational value of the attention to education has long been apparent. Its importance was clear to William James, the so-called 'father of American psychology', writing in 1890:

> **The faculty of voluntarily bringing back a wandering attention, over and over again, is the very root of judgment, character, and will. No one is *compos sui* (master of himself) if he have it not. An education which should improve this faculty would be the education par excellence. But it is easier to define this ideal than to give practical directions for bringing it about.**

William James, (1961) Psychology: Briefer Course, p. 424 Harper Torchbook.

James would perhaps be pleased that modern mindfulness is finally discovering ways to deliver the 'par excellence' education he thought was a pipe dream.

A new relationship with the mind - in the body and in the world

Modern science is demonstrating the wisdom of the ancient insight that mind and body are profoundly connected and that the separation of them in Western thinking is unhelpful. The mind and body have vast capacities, most of which we do not use as effectively as we might, especially as we get older and our horizons can narrow.

Mindfulness is often talked of as a 'mind training', but the practices that cultivate mindfulness include those that are founded in our immediate sensory experience of the body. Practices include resting our awareness on the changing sensations of the breath, body scan (moving the awareness through the parts of the body), sensory practice such as focusing on the detail of the taste and touch, the sensations of mindful eating, and awareness of the body in motion through mindful movement and mindful walking.

Over time we become more aware and sensitive to our bodies and their sensations, just as we become more aware of the quality and the shifting nature of our thoughts and feelings. Our appreciation grows of the profound interconnectedness between body sensations, emotions, thoughts and behaviour. We become more aware of the interrelatedness of all our experience, communicated to us through our mind and body and in response to our own actions and our experience of the outside world.

Stepping back from thoughts

Mindfulness practice can help us relate better to our thoughts, emotions and bodily states, including anger, worry, pain and discomfort, by intentionally 'stepping back' to observe them with kindness and curiosity as they play out in the mind and body, rather than getting caught up in them. This ability can help many of our reflective processes by showing us more clearly what our minds and bodies are doing. In the process we become more able to:

- choose and move flexibly between different mind and body states, and

- direct the mind down the paths we choose to go down, including those that help us feel more compassion towards ourselves and others.

More than calmness and relaxation – it's cultivating a new relationship with our experience

Mindfulness is commonly understood and promoted, particularly in schools, as a 'toolkit' for emotional regulation, a set of calming and relaxing techniques to use when we experience stress and difficult emotions. These aspects of mindfulness practice are easily grasped, a powerful and very real help, a practical starting point for most people, and highly attractive to schools.

However, without a deeper appreciation of some of the more subtle ways mindfulness works, naïve reliance on mindfulness as simply a relaxation and calming technique can backfire. It can lead to disillusionment when, as is inevitable, mindfulness fails to 'work immediately and reliably, usually followed by the student giving up. Mindfulness practice is inevitably challenging at some point. In a recent study[4] two thirds of the 84 school teachers who studied mindfulness reported 'unpleasant' experiences, although these were mostly not seen as serious, and some saw them as an opportunity for learning.

WHAT IS MINDFULNESS?

The model of mindfulness as a 'toolkit' to calm ourselves misses the deeper transformative and unique contribution mindfulness can make, which is to relate to our experience differently. Over time, as we learn simply to be with what is, we gradually develop the ability to be open-minded, curious, equanimous, non-judgemental, and kind about whatever we experience, be it pleasant, difficult or just neutral. We notice how we try to hang on to pleasant mind and body states, and attempt to push away and suppress difficult ones, and how this can in fact add to our distress. The, somewhat paradoxical, outcome is that by being with the difficult we do indeed experience more moments of calmness and relaxation, a greater ability to manage our emotions, and kinder and more-rational thoughts, including in the face of increasing levels of difficulty. We welcome these pleasant states fully, but without clinging to them in ways that then become a further source of tension. We develop greater insight into ourselves and our habitual reactions, which opens the door to new, more skilful possibilities, including the ability to take wise action a more helpful outcome than any 'quick fix.

Core values: cultivating compassion, kindness, and a social ethic

Mindfulness has never, by definition, been value free: a thief who practised attention-focusing skills, fully present in the here and now, to improve their craft would not be mindful as they would fail to approach the task with the core attitude of kindness. In order for an approach to properly be called 'mindfulness' the attitudes and values we bring to the practice, such as curiosity, care, and open-mindedness, are fundamental and non-negotiable.

> **Young people can quickly find a toolkit to calm down, to focus, to concentrate, to understand what stress is. And they are learning to be ok when it's not ok.**
>
> Jo Price, University of Kent Academies Trust

Practitioners, such as the renowned philosopher and contemplative Mathieu Ricard, have suggested that mindfulness practice is a vital starting point, and that we also need to take further explicit and active steps to cultivate our values and attitudes through meditative practices that explicitly encourage compassion, and ultimately through the whole way we live out lives.[5] The study of compassion, and associated practical training, is now growing apace. The two areas have started to merge over the last decade, with a number of mindfulness-based compassion courses now available.[6]

There is a growing sense within the world of mindfulness that mindfulness must not just be about helping us as individuals to succeed in our lives, but needs actively to help us cultivate the prosocial and ethical values that lead to the strengthening of our concern for others, and to living with a sense of interpersonal and ecological connectedness.[7]

> **Mindfulness is not a tool or instrument to get something else - whether that something is healing, success, wealth or winning. True mindfulness is a path, an ethical way of living, and every step along that path can already bring happiness, freedom and wellbeing, to ourselves and others. Happiness and wellbeing are not an individual matter. We interact with all people and all species.**
>
> Thich Nhat Hanh, from Happy Teachers Change the World: A Guide to Cultivating Mindfulness in Schools by Thich Nhat Hanh and Katherine Weare

WHAT IS MINDFULNESS?

A human capacity that underlies our happiness

Mindfulness is a natural, human capacity that can be developed through practice. It is not an esoteric experience: most of us have experienced an analogous present-moment mind state from time to time, for example, when fully present in a conversation, immersed in a hobby, or piece of music, or out in nature, or during a life-changing moment, or a peak experience. Mindfulness can help us be more in the present moment at will, more often and more sustainably, particularly during the mundane business of our daily lives, when we so easily slip back to autopilot, and which then so often in turn slides to negativity and passivity. Mindfulness essentially returns us to our lives.

> **Many of the practices have found their way into my everyday life; this morning as I set out for a walk, I decided not to use my headphones but just to walk mindfully and enjoy the moment by being fully present to it.**

Saqib Safdar, Teacher, Star Academies

Some now, fairly, definitive work based on the so-called 'science of happiness',[8] which attempts to explore what makes people authentically happy, suggests that the kinds of skills and attitudes that mindfulness cultivates can contribute to happiness. The evidence suggests that beyond a certain basic point happiness is not about ever more material goods or success. We feel happier and more at ease with ourselves when we feel more connected with others and our social environment, when we are feeling more in the moment, and when we are more open hearted, grateful, compassionate, trusting, caring and generous.

Mindfulness practice can be the antidote to the modern condition

We cannot just decide to be, and then remain, mindful and compassionate. Mindfulness may be a human trait, but it is not easy for any of us, young or old, to sustain in the face of our increasingly busy and stressful lives and in the face of modern social forces, any more than we can just decide to be physically fit in the face of pressures to lead a sedentary lifestyle. We are also operating with some now unhelpful hard-wired evolutionary tendencies. They include negativity bias[9] (the tendency to always be on the look-out for threats and dangers) and an inbuilt threat system[10] that is easily triggered, along with the stress response of fight, flight and freeze. These inherent human traits may once have enabled our genes to survive in physically hostile environments, but they no longer entirely stand us in good stead in a complex world built on social interaction and the need for cooperation.

The need to nurture a mindful way of being is arguably ever more urgent now when our digital world is feeding some of our inbuilt impulses and taking us towards some unhealthy states such as permanent distraction, literal addiction to our devices,[11] hypervigilance (such as 'fear of missing out'), constant comparison, snap judgments and social polarisation. In the face of some now somewhat dysfunctional inbuilt biological tendencies and modern pressures, it can help to turn to an antidote — the techniques developed by mindfulness practitioners over many millennia — to help cultivate the ability to summon and sustain a more present, open-minded, connected and caring state of being. This evolutionary mechanism which soothes us and connects us to others is also inherent within us if we give it a chance to flourish.[12]

Preserving the natural mindfulness of childhood?

Many of us recall early childhood as a time when we were more fully 'there' and present in mind and body in the moments of our lives, with heightened senses, more open-minded, more accepting of new experiences and of others unlike ourselves, more curious, more creative. Sadly, most of us tend to lose this innate capacity as we get older and in the face of growing demands and worries, encouragements to multi-task, and the potential distractions, false facts and social divisiveness that come from over reliance on digital technology. Competition-based, target-driven, schooling would seem to contribute to this sense of pressure.

Introducing mindfulness practice in schools can provide an opportunity to value, preserve, nurture and sustain these life-affirming states of mind in children, while enabling adults to partly reclaim them.

WHAT IS MINDFULNESS?

Some further myths and misconceptions about mindfulness

We have explored a few myths and misunderstandings already in this chapter, such as the belief that mindfulness is all about relaxation, or calm, or emptying the mind; here we outline a few frequently found in educational contexts.

> 'Mindfulness practice just means following the breath'

Although learning to pay attention to the breath is a core and powerful practice, it is just one practice, not the aim. It is not suitable for everyone, such as those with breathing difficulties, who can be helped to find other 'anchors' such as the sense of the body in contact with the floor and the chair, or an external focus such as sound.

> 'Mindfulness sounds good! I can use it to quieten unruly kids'

The young often find mindfulness practice calming and choose to use it themselves for self-regulation to manage difficult feelings and resist impulses.

There have been well-publicised examples of 'where meditation replaces detention' in which schools send students to quiet and calming places in which they learn meditation skills, instead of to detention rooms as a form of punishment. These approaches have been said to go down well with the school community and help transform attitudes.[13] Meditation could certainly be a useful part of a well considered and well monitored strategy which offers meditation to troubled and troublesome young people in a spirit of kindness, empathy and the positive teaching of skills.

However, there are dangers. Thoughtlessly using mindfulness as a sanction for an unruly class, as part of a punitive response to behaviour, as a form of immediate disciplinary action or to instruct students who are acting up to 'calm down and be mindful' would go against its fundamental open-minded, invitational ethic. Not least it would also almost certainly put them off the whole enterprise!

> 'Mindfulness is a panacea for all ills'

There has been a degree of 'hype' and overselling of mindfulness particularly in the popular media.[14] Those involved in disseminating mindfulness practice are clear it is not a magic bullet, and it is not for everyone or helpful at all times - some people simply do not take to it, and many people find it hard to sustain after initial enthusiasm. A balanced and evidence-based view is that good-quality authentic mindfulness teaching, including meditation, taught at the right time and place to the right people within a supportive context and as part of a broader set of actions is likely to have long-term beneficial effects.

> 'Mindfulness is religious, Buddhism by the back door'

Mindfulness is at root a human capacity, not a religious practice, and is today most often cultivated through approaches that don't make any reference to religious thinking or terminology, especially within education.

> 'Extracting mindfulness from its original spiritual origins means it lacks an ethic, it has become commodified, and is coercive, teaching people passively to accept the unacceptable'

There is now a whole critique of modern secular mindfulness as having been 'commodified' when it was separated from what was originally a whole spiritual ethic and social ethic; it is now no more than a set of superficial techniques used to manage stress. It has become a tool for 'the system' to help people become more 'resilient' and thus passively accept situations they should resist. This vision of mindfulness has been given the catchy name McMindfulness.[15]

This critique is a useful warning bell for us all to work together to ensure that this is not how mindfulness is used. The critique does not however fairly reflect the complex reality of how quality mindfulness is generally delivered in UK workplaces and schools, where there is growing recognition that we need to ensure that we operate with a full understanding of what mindfulness is, and ensure that it is not about encouraging compliance and the acceptance of toxic levels of stress. The sister guide to this one 'Building the case for mindfulness in the workplace' by The Mindfulness Initiative contains helpful case studies on the role of mindfulness in some leading edge companies, transforming corporate settings towards self-care, kindness and ethical corporate behaviour. Approaches to mindfulness in education are developing which help the young to become active citizens and critical thinkers, and build a sense of connection with one another, with society and with the planet.[16] This version of mindfulness is the starting point for this guidance.

PART TWO

DOES MINDFULNESS WORK – AND IF SO, HOW?

CHAPTER 2

The outcomes of mindfulness: a summary

Summary of Chapter 2

This chapter summarises the evidence from a growing number of systematic reviews and meta-analyses of the impacts of mindfulness on teachers and school-aged youth. (Chapter 3 and Chapter 4 unpack this evidence in more detail and with illustrative case studies.) Taken overall, the evidence shows that:

- Mindfulness is a foundational capacity which cultivates many interrelated aspects of mental and physical wellbeing in teachers and school students.

- Positive outcomes for teachers include improved psycho-social and physical wellbeing, improved self-care, a reduction in mental health problems (including depression and stress) and an improvement in their effectiveness as teachers.

- Positive outcomes for children and young people include improved psycho-social and physical health and wellbeing, reduced mental health problems (including stress and depression), and improved social and emotional skills, behaviour, cognition and learning and academic performance.

- Mindfulness is generally popular with children and young people, is effective for all age groups, and impacts equally on those with identified problems and those without. Adverse effects appear to be rare but the possibility needs to be looked for

- Systematic reviews and meta-analyses — academic articles that take the results of good-quality research papers and come to overall conclusions using careful and clear methods of selection and analysis — are the best guide to good-quality evidence.

THE OUTCOMES OF MINDFULNESS

WHAT – IN SUMMARY – DOES THE EVIDENCE SHOW?

Mindfulness is foundational

Although in the detail that follows, we look at outcomes separately, the growing evidence base of empirical research is making clear that mindfulness is a foundational capacity which can support many aspects of mental and physical wellbeing in teachers and school students simultaneously. It appears to work by strengthening some of the core mechanisms which underpin human flourishing, including the ability to focus the attention, to step back from the thinking process, and to develop the capacity for exercising emotion regulation and self-regulation. We explore these mechanisms in more detail in Chapter 5.

Mindfulness shows a wide range of positive outcomes for teachers

The evidence from systematic reviews and meta-analyses shows an overall picture of clearly positive impacts from Mindfulness-Based Interventions (MBIs), drawing specifically on research with teachers, on a range of interrelated outcomes.

- Psycho-social wellbeing including a sense of meaning and purpose, resilience, optimism, connectedness, happiness, and fulfilment.

- Physical health and wellbeing including heart rate, blood pressure, stress hormones, sleep quality and days absent from school.

- Mental health problems including reducing and helping prevent depression, stress, anxiety and burnout.

- Teacher effectiveness in areas which include improved emotion regulation, self-regulation, and metacognition, compassion, empathy, relationship building, clarity, priority setting, focus, staying on task, and relating effectively to student behaviour. It all leads to the ability to create effective and connected classrooms, school culture and ethos.

- Adverse effects are rare but need to be looked out for.

The nature of the evidence for teachers:

- The evidence for teachers is based on five published systematic reviews of mindfulness for teachers, two of which include a meta-analysis.

- These reviews draw together the results of an increasing number of individual studies of mindfulness for teachers – 30 individual studies were identified by the most recent 2018 meta-analysis as being of high enough quality to include.[17]

- These findings on outcomes for teachers specifically are in line with evidence from systematic reviews and meta-analyses of the outcomes of research on MBIs for working adults in general.[18]

- We explain the terms 'systematic review' and 'meta-analysis' towards the end of the chapter.

- We list all the systematic reviews and meta-analyses and their main results in Appendix 2.

> **RESEARCH EVIDENCE**
> **Mindfulness in schools scores exceptionally highly for acceptability**
>
> A 70–80% average rating for acceptability for MBIs is considerably higher than the average 50% acceptability score for new elements of the curriculum in primary-aged children in the UK, as shown in a report by the Department for Education (2011).
>
> *https://www.gov.uk/government/publications/framework-for-the-national-curriculum-a-report-by-the-expert-panel-for-the-national-curriculum-review*

Mindfulness shows a wide range of positive outcomes for children and young people in school contexts

The evidence from systematic reviews and meta-analyses shows an overall picture of a positive impact from MBIs on a range of interrelated outcomes.

- Psycho-social wellbeing including improving resilience, optimism, connectedness, and happiness.

- Physical health and wellbeing including heart rate, blood pressure, stress hormones, sleep quality, and days absent from school.

- Mental health problems including reducing and helping prevent depression, stress and anxiety

The Mindfulness Initiative / Implementing Mindfulness in Schools

THE OUTCOMES OF MINDFULNESS

- Social and emotional skills including improving self-regulation, emotion regulation, resilience, self-concept, empathy, compassion, kindness, and relationship skills.

- Behaviour problems including reducing aggression, hostility and symptoms of Attention Deficit Hyperactivity Disorder (ADHD).

- Cognition and learning in children, including attention, metacognition and self-regulation.

- Academic performance in children and young people in schools, including standardised achievement tests, measures of content mastery, test scores and grades.

- No human activity is totally risk free but there is as yet no evidence of serious adverse effects of MBIs with the young. Research is increasingly on the look out for such effects, to safeguard the needs of the vulnerable.

The nature of the evidence for children and young people:

- The evidence for children and young people is based on ten published systematic reviews of MBIs for school students, of which five include a meta-analysis.

- These reviews draw together the results of an increasing number of individual studies of mindfulness for the young. Around 60 individual studies were identified in a recent systematic review/meta-analysis in 2017[19] as being of high enough quality to include. Thirty-five of these studies used control groups; 30 of them are randomised control trials.

- We explain the terms 'systematic review' and 'meta-analysis' towards the end of the chapter.

- We list all the systematic reviews and meta-analyses and main results in Appendix 2.

Other significant findings

- MBIs are generally acceptable and popular with teachers, children and young people.

- MBIs can be effective for all ages of children and young people.

- MBIs for children in schools appear to impact equally well on those with problems (targeted approach) and on the whole school population (universal approaches).

KEY ISSUE
How to read the evidence

The most trustworthy and sound evidence in any field is found in studies published in scientific peer-reviewed journals of high standing. Getting a paper published is hard to do, it invariably requires rounds of corrections, and many are rejected by the experts who review them.

Once a field such as mindfulness has developed it is best not to rely on reading just one paper as the results of any individual study can be misleading and not fit with the general trend. Relying on reviews is a safer option.

There are now enough individual studies of mindfulness in schools to bring together two types of robust review:

- Systematic reviews carefully sift the evidence from individual studies and come to conclusions based on studies selected using clear and transparent quality criteria for inclusion and exclusion.

- Meta-analyses build on a systematic review and add a further stage of estimating what the overall statistics suggest about the strength and certainty of the outcomes.

Systematic reviews and meta-analyses are generally used by policy-makers in guiding decisions. In this guidance we use the overall conclusions from systematic reviews and meta-analyses whenever possible, illustrating with case studies from good-quality papers published in peer-reviewed journals.

Take care! Online evidence and reports in popular media are unfiltered, may be misreported and should be approached with scepticism. Online unpublished evaluation reports by programmes themselves may be helpful, but remember that they have not been subjected to peer review.

THE OUTCOMES OF MINDFULNESS

KEY ISSUE
A pyramid of evidence

A so called 'hierarchy of evidence' is often used to guide public policy. It suggests that as we ascend the pyramid the more statistically based methods create greater levels of reliability and generalisability. It is helpful but should be used with caution. The qualitative work towards the base of the pyramid is vital to build a solid base of understanding, without which numerically based work can be meaningless. We explore the value of both quantitative and qualitative enquiry in evaluation in Chapter 10

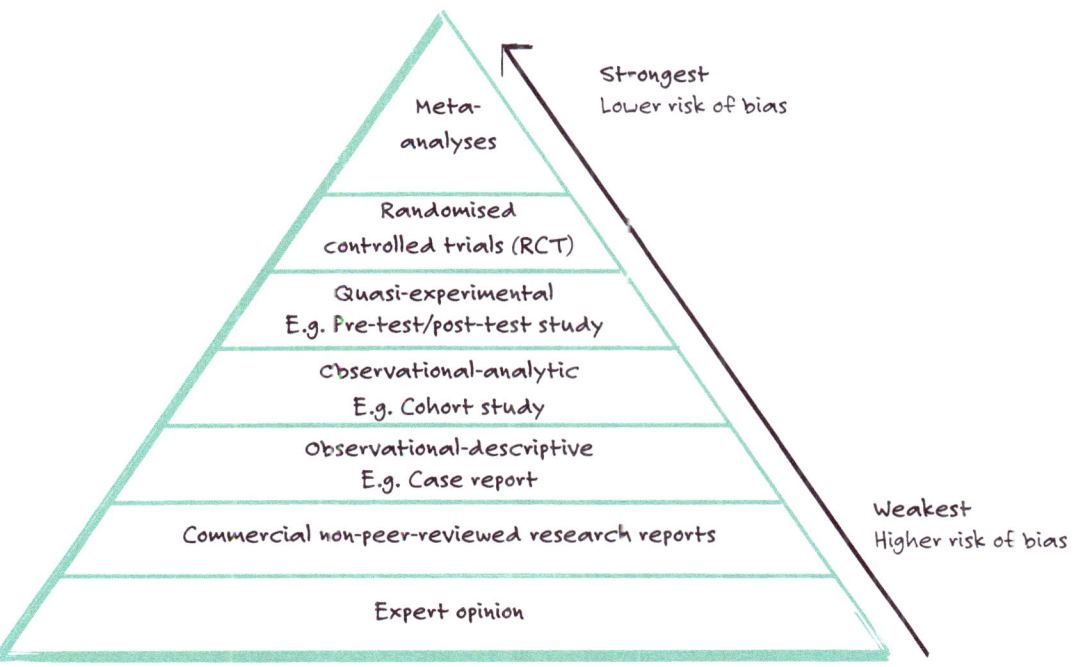

EXPLORE FURTHER
Further advice on understanding the research base

A useful repository of current research papers and reviews is curated by the Mindfulness in Schools Project: https://mindfulnessinschools.org/the-evidence-base/.

There is a useful 'toolbox' on 'keeping up with the scientific evidence' in the Fieldbook for Mindfulness Innovators: https://www.themindfulnessinitiative.org/fieldbook-for-mindfulness-innovators.

CHAPTER 3

The outcomes of mindfulness for teachers

Summary of Chapter 3

This chapter reviews in more detail the evidence for the outcomes of Mindfulness-Based Interventions (MBIs) for teachers summarised in Chapter 2, and illustrates the themes with brief case study examples of good-quality research on MBIs for school teachers. It concludes that the balance of evidence shows that when MBIs are well conducted, they show the following outcomes.

- MBIs can improve many aspects of teacher psycho-social wellbeing, including a sense of meaning and efficacy, self-care and self-compassion, and physical health.

- MBIs can help reduce teacher mental health problems, including burnout, depression, stress and anxiety.

- MBIs can help teachers be more effective, improve their skills of self-regulation, including their abilities to pay attention and be in the moment, stand back from their thoughts and manage their emotions and their reactions, and respond more skilfully to students they may be finding difficult and in times of stress.

- Teachers who engage in MBIs are generally more effective in the classroom, being better able to focus on concepts and processes rather than on content and behaviour management, to stay on task, and resist distraction.

- Teachers who engage in MBIs generally relate more effectively to student behaviour, with more empathy and presence, and create calmer and more focused classroom environments.

- No human activity is without risk, and serious adverse effects currently appear to be fairly uncommon, but care needs to be taken to look for such effects, to safeguard as much as possible, and to manage the expectations of those undertaking mindfulness.

WELLBEING

What is 'wellbeing' in research terms?

Wellbeing is a term that is steadily gaining traction in schools. When used in health and social research, the term 'wellbeing' is a multi-dimensional concept that attempts to capture the overall quality and balance of a person's physical, mental, and social life. Wellbeing includes a sense of physical vitality, thriving, purpose and meaning, and the leading of a worthwhile, fulfilled, engaged, caring, and socially connected life.[20]

The rise in popularity of the concept of wellbeing reflects a new emphasis on the positive in studies of human development, replacing the long-term focus in health and the social sciences on negativity, problems and pathologies in traditional approaches.

Can wellbeing be measured?

Wellbeing can be a vague term, but scales have been developed which attempt to assess it with a degree of clarity and precision. Wellbeing scales are often used in educational research, including in the evaluation of mindfulness, and include items which refer to states such as satisfying interpersonal relationships, connection with others, cheerfulness, optimism, relaxation, clarity of thinking, and a sense of meaning, social usefulness, agency and purpose. It generally includes aspects of physical health and wellbeing. We suggest how a school might use these wellbeing scales to evaluate the impacts of mindfulness on wellbeing in their own school in Chapter 5 and list some of the most popular in Appendix 3.

Teachers' wellbeing

The evidence for the impact of mindfulness on teacher wellbeing is totally clear. All six systematic reviews including the most recent meta-analysis[21] by Hwang et al. (2017),[22] which included 16 controlled studies of MBIs for school staff, determined impacts on many aspects of positive wellbeing, including physical health, self-

> **My top suggestion? Put staff wellbeing at the top of your agenda. Start with the adults!**

Lynburn Primary School, Fife

regulation, and a sense of efficacy. The review concluded that *'Effects of mindfulness-based interventions on teachers' wellbeing and performance demonstrate positive relations with participation in mindfulness practice. Those who practise mindfulness are better for it'.*

The evidence of the impact of MBIs with respect to teachers is supported by research on mindfulness in the working population more generally. Two recent meta-analyses suggest that mindfulness for working adults can reliably improve physical and mental health, reduce job-related stress and absenteeism, and improve work-related satisfaction, usually with between small and medium, but sometimes large, effect sizes.[23] [24]

There is increasing emphasis on the need for mindfulness research not to be complacent and to look out for adverse effects. No human activity is without risks and side effects, and the evidence suggests serious adverse effects from mindfulness are rare.[25] However in a recent study with 84 school teachers, two-thirds of participants reported unpleasant experiences. Most thought these were not serious, and some found them useful for learning. The authors concluded that this *'highlighted the need to manage expectations about benefits and difficulties that may occur in mindfulness-based programs and to work skilfully with participants experiencing difficulties'.* [26]

Impacts on teachers' physical health and wellbeing

Modern mindfulness originated in the world of physical health: Jon Kabat-Zinn was working at Massachusetts Medical Hospital, where he developed his original eight-

> **Teaching the skills of wellbeing brings humanity back to education, it can rekindle teachers' passion for educating young people and it can restore the innate meaning and purpose to teaching that comes from wanting to make a difference in young people's lives.**

Adrian Bethune, Wellbeing in the Primary Classroom

THE OUTCOMES OF MINDFULNESS FOR TEACHERS

> ❝ The search procedures led to the identification of 18 manuscripts that included a total sample of 1,001 educators. Mindfulness-based interventions were found to have significant positive effects across all domains. Mindfulness-based interventions resulted in large effects on feelings of mindfulness, moderate effects for decreases in stress and anxiety, and small effects on feelings of depression and burnout.

Zarate et al. (2018)

week Mindfulness-Based Stress Reduction (MBSR) course to help patients with physical health conditions, particularly pain, whose symptoms were proving intractable for the treatments available.[27] Since that time MBSR has been subjected to many evaluations, including of its impacts on physical health, with generally positive results.[28] Mindfulness has been shown to impact on a wide range of indicators of physical health, including chronic pain, fatigue, sleep, heart disease and an enhanced immune system, on addictive behaviour and even on the ageing process.[29]

There have been specific studies of the impact of mindfulness on the physical health of teachers, for example:

- A control trial by Jennings et al. in 2013 found a significant reduction in teachers' 'daily physical symptoms' of ill health after studying a short intensive course on mindfulness for teachers' self-care.[30]

- An RCT of 82 female teachers taught an eight-week mindfulness course showed that those who practiced more frequently after the course had lower blood pressure in response to a real-life stressful task compared with a control group who did not practice five months after the course.[31]

Self-compassion

Teachers regularly report that, as they work in an 'other-centred' profession, they feel they need permission to 'apply their own oxygen mask before helping others' and engaging in self-care. Research suggests they relate more strongly to the relational aspects of mindfulness than they do to the intra-personal (focus on the self), which is understandable but may need balancing.[32] A recent systematic review of mindfulness for teachers concluded that self-compassion is one of the underlying mechanisms that make mindfulness so impactful in many areas connected with wellbeing and effectiveness.[33]

Mindfulness helps address mental health problems in teachers

Mental health problems in teachers appear to be on the rise, and from an already alarmingly high baseline. In a context where workplace stress has generally reached epidemic proportions, stress in the teaching profession is considerably higher than the workplace average. Figures from the annual and well-respected 'Teacher Wellbeing Index' suggest that three-quarters of teachers experience work-related stress symptoms, with nearly half reporting depression, anxiety or panic attacks due to work.[34] At any one time more than half are considering leaving the profession due to poor health. These figures are even higher for senior leaders. There are known difficulties in recruitment, and high and expensive rates of attrition in trainee and practising teachers. Start the

---

RESEARCH EVIDENCE
Mindfulness impacts on teacher stress, wellbeing and self-compassion

Eighty-nine secondary school teachers and staff were taught the **Mindfulness in Schools Project .b Foundation Course** for teachers, through nine after-school sessions. They were divided into the same size intervention and control groups. Staff in the intervention group showed a significant reduction in their **stress, and significant increases in their wellbeing, mindfulness and self-compassion (lower self-judgment and increased self-kindness)** compared with the control group. The effect sizes were large for all four outcome measures.

Beshai, S., McAlpine, L., Weare, K., and Kuyken, W. (2015). A non-randomised feasibility trial assessing the efficacy of a mindfulness-based intervention for teachers to reduce stress and improve well-being. Mindfulness, 7(1), 198-208.

sentence with 'A recent report a recent report by Ofsted in 2019 echoed this dire picture, noting the stress caused by the workload and stress created by its own inspections.[35]

So, the growing and solid evidence that mindfulness can be of help in addressing teacher mental health problems, including stress, is welcome. Such work is in no way a replacement for active efforts to address the structural and systemic causes of teacher stress, and indeed mindfulness practice can often help those involved to see the causes more clearly and address them with more vigour.

All five systematic reviews deduced positive impacts on the reduction of mental health problems in teachers. A recent meta-analysis by Zarate et al. found positive impacts on burnout, depression, and stress from 18 studies on MBIs for teachers.[36] Similarly, a review by Lomas et al. based on 19 papers and nearly 2,000 participants found clear impacts on burnout, anxiety, depression and stress, as well as more positive wellbeing measures (e.g. life satisfaction).[37]

The evidence for these impacts is supported by a solid body of work with the adult population in general. The largest systematic review of mindfulness for working adults, by Khoury et al., based on 209 individual studies, concluded that mindfulness is an effective treatment for a variety of psychological problems and should be supported.[38] The NHS and NICE (the National Institute for Health and Care Excellence, who only operate on the highest quality evidence) recommend mindfulness as a preventative treatment for adults who have had three or more previous episodes of depression, but who are currently well.[39]

MINDFULNESS AND TEACHER EFFECTIVENESS

The quality of the teachers, and their skills and attitudes, are at the heart of any effective school, so impacts on teacher effectiveness is one of the most significant areas for the impacts of mindfulness.

Emotion regulation

A recent systematic review of 13 studies on MBIs for teachers by Emerson et al. concluded that emotion regulation is the area in which mindfulness for teachers *'showed strongest promise'*.[40] In qualitative work included in this review, teachers said emotion regulation is the aspect of MBIs they find most helpful, helping them to cultivate greater awareness and recognition of their emotions, including how they play out in the body, and the ability to manage their own reactions, including towards 'difficult' students and in times of stress.

In a recent systematic review of mindfulness for teachers, Hwang et al. concluded from six studies that teachers who engaged in mindfulness were better able to focus, prioritise, and resist distraction and unintended shifts in attention, including in the classroom.[41]

Changing relationship to experience

A systematic review of mindfulness for teachers, based on 16 studies, included some analysis of qualitative data collection.[42] It concluded that mindfulness reliably changes teachers' relationship to their experience, including their thoughts and emotions, which led to a wide range of beneficial impacts on teacher effectiveness.

- Teachers noticed that they had increased awareness of passing thoughts and associated emotions and body sensations. They came to recognise the inextricable links between these three facets of their experience, which also improved the quality of the experience. Their thought processes improved and they were able to take more effective action.

> **RESEARCH EVIDENCE**
> **Mindfulness increases teacher effectiveness in the classroom**
>
> A systematic review of 16 studies by Hwang et al. concluded that mindfulness helps teachers to create effective classrooms in many different ways.
>
> 'Mindfulness has positive effects on the in-service teachers' functioning in classroom organisation, emotion regulation, use of positive-affect words in classroom, along with their work and success in improving students' behavioural learning outcomes… Mindfulness activities …were found to be effective for creating calmer and more focused classroom environments. Practising mindfulness also was helpful for teachers in implementing lesson planning to engage students in learning. Key concepts were clarified, prioritised, simplified and delivered in engaging ways, using graphic organisers, stories and art. Teachers noticed their teaching had become more focused on the concepts and processes of student learning rather than, as previously, subject content and student behaviour.'
>
> *Quoted from Hwang, Y., Bartlett, B. Green, M., and Hand, K. (2017) A systematic review of mindfulness interventions for in-service teachers: A tool to enhance teacher wellbeing and performance. Teaching and Teacher Education, 64, 26-42.*

THE OUTCOMES OF MINDFULNESS FOR TEACHERS

- Teachers reported an increased ability to examine their perceptions and perspectives before reacting, which opened new possibilities of choice and action, including letting habitual and compulsive thoughts come and go, and attending to just one thing at a time.

Responding more effectively to student behaviour

In the next chapter we summarise the evidence for improvements in student behaviour through teachers learning mindfulness themselves. The review by Hwang et al. suggests that mindfulness can help cultivate the skills and attitudes that help teachers manage student behaviour more effectively.[43] To summarise the findings of the review:

- mindfulness impacts on how teachers perceive behaviour, helping them be less likely to view it negatively (for example as aimed at them, a threat or uncontrollable), and see it more positively (for example as meaningful and an opportunity for growth). Teachers report that this shift impacts on their ability to deal with behaviour more effectively and reduces their own levels of stress and exhaustion.

- mindfulness can also help teachers to support students more effectively in managing their behaviour. Teachers reported that regularly used mindfulness to address student conflict at school, and to ground their own and students' awareness through breathing, relaxing, and focusing on surroundings before talking about conflict.

- the cultivation of the attitudes of kindness and curiosity, and the skills of re-perceiving can lead teachers to view behaviour in more realistic, empathic and skilful ways. Teachers reported that they used mindfulness as a non-reactivity practice themselves for calming down before taking care of the situation and to demonstrate empathy and care for their students.

Creating effective and connected classroom climates

Teaching is at root a 'relational' occupation, founded on the ability to manage one's own emotions and behaviour, communicate effectively, motivate others, handle complex social situations including conflict, and make warm and authentic relationships. A systematic review of 16 studies by Hwang et al.[44] concluded that mindfulness helps create effective classrooms in several interconnected ways see the box on page 30.

RESEARCH EVIDENCE
Mindfulness shows a wide range of long-term benefits for teacher wellbeing and effectiveness

Two hundred and twenty-four teachers in 36 elementary public schools in New York City in the United States followed the **Cultivating Awareness and Resilience in Education (CARE for Teachers) programme.** This is a 30-hour mindfulness-based professional development programme designed to promote the social and emotional competence of teachers of all ages and improve the quality of classroom interactions.

CARE has been the subject of five published studies. In this, the largest quantitative study, published in 2017, the efficacy of the programme was assessed using a cluster randomised controlled trial. Teachers completed self-report measures and assessments of their participating students, and their classrooms were systematically observed and assessed by blinded researchers.

Teachers showed statistically significant **direct positive effects with respect to adaptive emotion regulation, mindfulness, and psychological distress** compared with controls. **CARE classrooms were more productive and more emotionally positive, and the teachers demonstrated greater sensitivity to their students' needs**, compared with classrooms of teachers in the control group. A follow-up found that teachers who participated in CARE reported both **sustained and new benefits for their own wellbeing and their teaching nearly a year after the intervention.**

Jennings, P.A., Brown, J.L., Frank, J.L., Doyle, S., Oh, Y., Davis, R., Greenberg, M.T. (2017). Impacts of the CARE for Teachers programme on teachers' social and emotional competence and classroom interactions. Journal of Educational Psychology, 109(7), 1010-1028.

CHAPTER 4

The outcomes of mindfulness for children and young people

Summary of Chapter 4

This chapter reviews in more detail the evidence for the outcomes of Mindfulness-Based Interventions (MBIs) for children and young people in school settings summarised in Chapter 2. It concludes that:

- MBIs impact on many aspects of student psycho-social wellbeing, including positive mood, self-efficacy, empathy and connectedness, across all age ranges.

- MBIs impact on aspects of physical wellbeing in the young including blood pressure, heart rate, cortisol, and improvements in sleep.

- MBIs help reduce student mental health problems including burnout, depression, and stress with emerging evidence for impacts on anxiety, trauma, and eating and sleep disorder.

- Mindfulness impacts on social and emotional skills including positive self-concept, the skills of self-management including emotional recognition and emotional literacy emotion regulation, resilience, motivation, optimism and persistence, and on the relational skills of sociability, caring, empathy, and compassion.

- MBIs impact on aspects of learning and cognition including self-regulation, executive function, attention and focus, metacognition, and cognitive flexibility.

- There is a small amount of emerging evidence of impacts on academic performance and results on tests of achievement, and on grade scores.

- There is a small amount of emerging evidence for impacts on behaviour, including in students with ADHD.

THE OUTCOMES OF MINDFULNESS FOR CHILDREN AND YOUNG PEOPLE

> **RESEARCH EVIDENCE**
> **Mindfulness is foundational for school students' skills, capacities and flourishing**
>
> Mindfulness is a foundational capacity because it can support many aspects of mental and physical wellbeing and performance simultaneously. This case study illustrates the breadth of interrelated areas fundamental to education, and to human flourishing, in which just one MBI in a school setting can demonstrate benefits.
>
> Ninety-nine children aged 9 to 10 in Canada were taught MindUP, a programme and curriculum that combines mindfulness, gratitude practice, social and emotional learning and neuroscience education. The programme in the US and Canada has published several outcome evaluations and process evaluations on implementation. This was a study of the 12-week version. The study was a randomised control trial. The programme was assessed by self-report, teacher report, tests of performance and peer ratings.
>
> - The children who experienced the MBI reported improvements in their social and emotional skills including optimism, emotional control, empathy, perspective taking, prosocial goals, and mindful attention, compared with the control group.
>
> - The children reported fewer depressive symptoms, compared with the control group, who demonstrated significant deterioration in these measures during the time frame of the study.
>
> - Peer report suggested improvements in sociality, with significant improvements in sharing, trustworthiness, helpfulness, and taking others' perspectives, and significant decreases in aggressive behaviour.
>
> - There were improvements in academic learning, with a significant increase in self-reported 'school self-concept' (i.e. perceived academic abilities and interest and enjoyment) and a 15% gain in teacher-reported maths achievement.
>
> - Tests of students' performance on various tasks suggested they had improved aspects of self-regulation and executive function, with significantly shorter response times but sustained accuracy and better selective attention, compared with those in the control group.
>
> Schonert-Reichl, K. A., Oberle, E., Lawlor, M. S., Abbott, D., Thomson, K., Oberlander, T. F., & Diamond, A. (2015). Enhancing cognitive and social-emotional development through a simple-to-administer mindfulness-based school program for elementary school children: A randomized controlled trial. Developmental Psychology, 51, 52–66.

The wellbeing of children and young people in schools

Student wellbeing is increasingly on the agenda of schools, the inspectorate, and educational policy-makers. We summarised what is meant by wellbeing in research terms in the previous chapter, emphasising that it is a multi-dimensional and positive concept that refers to the quality and balance of a person's life, and to a sense of joy, thriving and purpose, and which can to some extent be measured by the kind of validated scales we include in Appendix 3.

The shift towards an interest in student wellbeing has been helped by the clear evidence of the symbiosis between wellbeing and the learning and attainment agenda, and the growing recognition that both agendas work best when both are present and actively support each other.[45]

The impact of mindfulness on student wellbeing

The impact of mindfulness on student wellbeing is clear and well proven. Ten systematic reviews of mindfulness and the young, listed in Appendix 2, found small, and occasionally medium, effects on signs of positive wellbeing in school-aged children in almost all the studies that measured wellbeing or the factors that contribute to it (measures of wellbeing are often part of instruments that measure mental health and/or social skills). Impacts were found on psycho-social indicators such as positive mood, self-efficacy, empathy and connectedness, and across all age ranges.

> **RESEARCH EVIDENCE**
> **Mindfulness increases student wellbeing and sense of connection.**
>
> One hundred and twenty-four children aged 9-12 in three schools in New Zealand studied an eight-lesson module, tailored to fit with their cultural Maori attitudes to health and wellbeing. Practices included mindfulness, plus the cultivation of kindness and gratitude, emotion-regulation and a sense of interconnectedness with the wider environment including nature.
>
> There was a significant increase in students' subjective wellbeing, cheerfulness, satisfying interpersonal relationships, and in indicators of mindfulness. Changes in mindfulness in individual students were positively related to changes in wellbeing.
>
> *Bernay, R. Graham, E. Devcich, D.D. Rix, G. and Rubie-Davies, C.M. 'Pause, breathe, smile: a mixed-methods study of student wellbeing following participation in an eight-week, locally developed mindfulness program in three New Zealand schools', Advances in School Mental Health Promotion, DOI:10.1080/1754730X.2016.1154474 2016.*

The evidence base for the impact of mindfulness on physical health in school-aged students is smaller than that for adults, but there are some positive results emerging. A systematic review in 2016 summarised the impacts of mindfulness on the physical health of children and young people from six published studies of MBIs, four of them RCTs.[46] They showed evidence on a range of indicators of physical health including systolic and diastolic blood pressure, on heart rate, on urinary sodium excretion rate and on reductions in levels of cortisol (both indicators of a reduction in stress) and improvements in sleep.

Mindfulness helps address mental health problems in young people

A reason schools often turn to mindfulness is a concern with the growing mental health problems of those they teach. The statistics are familiar but alarming.[47] Around 25% of children and young people have an identifiable mental health disorder, with 10% needing specialist treatment. Problems are occurring at an ever earlier age, with 50% of problems established before the age of 15 and 75% by age 24.[48] Yet three-quarters of young people who are experiencing mental health problems are not receiving treatment and, right across the age span, most mental health problems remain untreated.

The situation appears to be worsening,[49] and in the face of what is clearly a rising wave of need and severely limited funding for specialist services, schools are being asked to bridge the gap and step up to this challenge in ways that are very new to them. Coping with this rising level of difficulty also has knock-on effects on teacher stress and sense of overwhelm. Any positive contribution mindfulness might make is welcome.

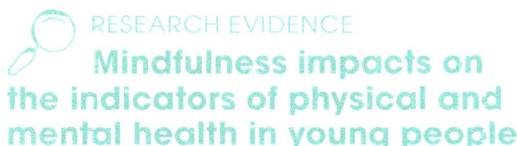

> **The best part about doing mindfulness was that it ended up helping me with my over thinking and my stressing out before exams.**
>
> *Secondary student*

> **RESEARCH EVIDENCE**
> **Mindfulness impacts on the indicators of physical and mental health in young people**
>
> Forty-two boys aged 11–12 in a small school for a low-income urban neighbourhood in the US, 95% of whom were African American, studied a 12-week programme closely based on the MBSR programme. **Cortisol levels (the 'stress hormone') increased during the school term for the control group participants but remained constant for MBSR participants.** The intervention group also showed less anxiety and improved coping skills, assessed by self-report.
>
> *Sibinga, E. M. S., Perry-Parrish, C., Chung, S., Johnson, S. B., Smith, M., and Ellen, J. M. (2013). 'School-based mindfulness instruction for urban male youth: A small randomized controlled trial'. Preventive Medicine, 57(6): 799–801*

THE OUTCOMES OF MINDFULNESS FOR CHILDREN AND YOUNG PEOPLE

A recent systematic review of mindfulness and the young concluded that impacts on mental health form the most robust evidence for mindfulness.[50] A strong set of reviews and evaluations of MBIs and the young show impacts on levels of depression and stress from a sizeable number of studies, with further promising emerging evidence for impacts on anxiety, trauma, eating and sleep disorders from a smaller number of studies.

- The strongest impacts appear to be on the mental health of older adolescents.

- The evidence on whether mindfulness has more impact on those with more severe problems is currently mixed and, supports the case for both universal and targeted approaches in schools, ideally working seamlessly together.

Cultivating social and emotional skills

Mental health is inextricably linked with the ability to exercise social and emotional skills, and the two areas overlap considerably. Social and emotional skills enable children and adults to understand and manage emotions, set and achieve positive goals, feel and show empathy for others, establish and maintain positive relationships, and make responsible decisions and take effective action. Extensive research has mapped a convincing link between social and emotional skills and success in most areas of life, including learning, school attainment and completion, earning potential, the prevention of mental health problems, less risky behaviour, and resilience.[51]

Mindfulness clearly impacts on social and emotional skills. The majority of evaluations of MBIs for school-aged children and young people have measured aspects of social and emotional skills and have generally found beneficial outcomes. A cluster of studies have shown impacts on children's self-image, self-acceptance[52], and the sense of a positive, proactive self-concept [53]. There is also reliable evidence for impact on the skills of self-management including emotion regulation, resilience, motivation, optimism and persistence, and on the relational skills of sociability, caring, empathy, and compassion. [54][55]

Several UK programmes now combine mindfulness with the teaching of social and emotional learning (SEL), an approach which is common in the US. Evaluations of this approach continue to add to accumulating evidence that this can be an impactful way forward. We explore this further in Chapter 4 on implementation.

There is an increasing focus in schools on whole school approaches to mental health and wellbeing and the central importance of school ethos, particularly a sense of 'school connectedness'. Social and emotional skills

> ### RESEARCH EVIDENCE
> ### Mindfulness impacts on the mental health and wellbeing of teenagers
>
> Five hundred and twenty-two students aged 12 to 16 in 12 secondary schools were taught the **nine-session UK Mindfulness in Schools Project .b programme for teens.** The students were divided into an intervention and a control group.
>
> Immediately after the intervention the only measure showing significant difference compared with controls was depressive symptoms but three months follow-up showed significant, statistically small, **changes in stress and depression and greater wellbeing**, suggesting a delayed effect (a phenomenon which has been observed quite frequently in mental health interventions). Three-month follow-up was timed to be examination time, the most stressful part of the school year, to test whether the MiSP curriculum conferred protection, which it appeared to do.
>
> **Those who engaged in more home practice showed greater wellbeing and less stress at follow-up**, a finding replicated in an earlier study of a four-week version of the programme by Huppert and Johnson.
>
> *Kuyken et al. (2013). Effectiveness of the Mindfulness in Schools Programme: Non-randomised controlled feasibility study. British Journal of Psychiatry, 203(2), 126-131. doi:10.1192/bjp.bp.113.126649*

> 66 **The best thing is that when my mum or dad are away and I miss them I can do a practice and I feel a bit better.**
>
> *Primary pupil*

RESEARCH EVIDENCE
Teaching about mindfulness plus kindness and gratitude impacts on children's social and cognitive functioning

Sixty-eight preschool children from seven classrooms across six schools in the US were taught the Kindness Curriculum as two 25-minute lessons over 12 weeks. It teaches mindfulness practice, aimed at cultivating attention and emotion regulation, with a shared emphasis on kindness practices (e.g., empathy, gratitude, sharing) and incorporates children's literature, music, and movement.

- The intervention group showed greater improvements in social competence and cognitive functioning, showed less selfish behaviour, and had higher grades for health and social-emotional development, compared with the control group.

- Children who had initially lower grades in social competence exhibited larger shifts.

Flook, L., Goldberg, S. B., Pinger, L., and Davidson, R. J. (2015). 'Promoting prosocial behaviour and self-regulatory skills in preschool children through a mindfulness-based kindness curriculum'. Developmental Psychology, 51(1): 44–51

---

are at the heart of this process, helping create a positive school ethos: where members of a school community actively cultivate and practise relational skills, where schools and classrooms are more 'prosocial' and genuinely inclusive, places in which all can feel safe, connected and thrive[56] socially, emotionally and educationally.

Mindfulness and compassion

Compassion, and related 'heartfulness' areas such as kindness and gratitude, is a growing focus within education. Some recent studies of MBIs for school students and for teachers have taught and measured improvements in new areas including the cultivation of gratitude and forgiveness. The boundaries between MBIs that focus more on the attentional components of mindfulness and those that also focus more extensively on compassion are becoming blurred. The box above illustrates the deep and wide impact of a 'kindness curriculum' which combined mindfulness and compassion.

Mindfulness helps me with concentrating and focusing better.

Primary pupil

Impacts on cognition, learning and attainment

Schools generally see their traditional core business as promoting learning and attainment, and although we may hope to widen this agenda, mindfulness will have more acceptance in mainstream education once its impacts in this area become more apparent. Teachers regularly report that one of the reasons they are introducing mindfulness into their schools is that they hope that it will improve student learning.[57]

RESEARCH EVIDENCE
Mindfulness impacts on children's metacognition, as well as their mood

'Seventy-one children aged 7–9 from three primary schools in the UK 'Mindfulness in Schools Project were taught the Paws b eight-week Primary School programme. Teacher reports of children's meta-cognitive abilities showed significant improvements at follow-up, with a large effect size, compared with the control group. There were also significant decreases in negative affect (emotion) at follow-up, with a large effect size.'

Vickery, C.E. and Dorjee, D. (2016) 'Mindfulness training in primary schools decreases negative affect and increases meta-cognition in children'. Frontiers in Psychology

THE OUTCOMES OF MINDFULNESS FOR CHILDREN AND YOUNG PEOPLE

Six systematic reviews and meta-analyses have looked at this area and found positive impacts on a range of aspects of learning and cognition in school-aged students. The most recent review bases its conclusions on 22 studies in this area.[58] Between them, these reviews deduced impacts on self-regulation, executive function, attention and focus, metacognition, and cognitive flexibility. These effects were especially apparent in those with greater difficulties in learning and cognition. These aspects of cognition are increasingly seen as underlying mechanisms that impact at a deep level across the whole of our mental processes, and we explore them further in Chapter 3, How does mindfulness work?

Impacts on academic performance

Five systematic reviews show some promising evidence of impacts on academic performance and results on tests of achievement and grade scores spread over a number of studies. Subjects which have shown evidence of impact include verbal creativity, language and literature, foreign languages, and philosophy[59][60], reading and science grades[61] and maths.[62]

Impacts on behaviour

There are not yet many studies that have measured impacts on student behaviour directly, but the most recent systematic review of mindfulness for school-aged students came to cautiously positive conclusions based on around five studies.[63] The review deduced small to medium impacts on aggression[64][65], hostility and impacts on Attention Deficit Hyperactivity Disorder (ADHD).[66]

This needs to be set alongside the recognition of the meaningfulness of so called 'difficult' behaviour, and mindfulness has a strong contribution to make to shifting the way 'difficult' behaviour is perceived and responded to by the adults involved, as we have suggested.

> **I am normally quite angry and this has helped me to calm down.**
>
> *Primary pupil*

RESEARCH EVIDENCE
Mindfulness impacts on attainment in school subjects

Sixty-one first-year high-school students, with a mean age of 16.3, were taught the Spanish mindfulness programme Meditación Fluir. It involved a one-and-a-half-hour session once a week for ten weeks with students then expected to practice daily for 30 minutes. This was an RCT, using a wait-list design.

Significant improvements were found in academic performance in Spanish language and literature, foreign languages, and philosophy (the three subjects examined). Students also improved their self-concept and reported reduced test-related anxiety.

Franco Justo, C., Mañas, I., Cangas, A. J., and Gallego, J. (2011). Exploring the effects of a mindfulness program for students of secondary school'. Int. J. Knowl. Soc. Res. 2: 14–28. doi: 10.4018/jksr.2011010102

RESEARCH EVIDENCE
Mindfulness impacts on student behaviour

Four hundred and nine children (83% enrolled in a California free lunch program and 95.7% from an ethnic minority group) attended, from kindergarten through sixth grade, a five-week mindfulness-based curriculum developed by the US Mindful Schools Programme. Children's skills were measured at pre-intervention, immediately post-intervention, and seven weeks post-intervention. Teachers reported improved classroom behaviour in terms of paying attention, self-control, participation in activities, and caring/respect for others, improvements which lasted up to seven weeks post-intervention.

Black, D. S., and Fernando, R. (2013). 'Mindfulness training and classroom behaviour among lower-income and ethnic minority elementary school children'. Journal of Child and Family Studies, 23(7), 1242–1246. https://www.ncbi.nlm.nih.gov/pmc/articles/PMC4304073/#APP1

RESEARCH EVIDENCE
Unexpected findings from a large scale RCT point to the need to scale up carefully

MYRIAD (My Resilience in Adolescence) was a large scale randomised control trial involving more than 28,000 young adolescents 650 teachers, and 100 schools. The curriculum chosen was an established and well researched one and had in a previous control trial showed impacts on pupils' stress, depression and wellbeing[i]. MYRIAD's stated aim was to discover whether "schools-based mindfulness training is an effective, cost-effective, accessible and scale-able way to promote mental health and wellbeing in adolescence."

As expected, teachers reported lower levels of burnout and improved school climate, with greater levels of respect across the school. However, and unexpectedly, the intervention was not better than normal PSHE lessons for pupils in terms of impacts on depression, or well-being. Pupil enjoyment was also unexpectedly mixed. The majority (80%) of young people did not do the required mindfulness practice homework, however those that did became more mindful and enjoyed better mental health.

A commentary document by the Mindfulness Initiative explored why the pupil results were not as expected and suggested that teacher selection may have been a key factor[ii]. The project's effort to explore scaleability was interpreted to mean that teachers and schools could only be selected for the trial if they had not shown an interest or involvement in mindfulness beforehand, in contrast to the usual well motivated and knowledgeable participants who opt for training. The average level of competence achieved by the teachers was 3/6, "advanced beginner"[iii], and teachers who fell below that level of basic competence to teach were still included in the data analysis. These lower than usual levels of motivation and competence may have been influential over the unexpectedly low impact. It is telling that in the trial the teachers who were judged to be the most skilled also had the highest rates of young people practicing and showing greater benefit. Scaling up needs to done with care.

Plain language summaries and links to the academic papers that have emerged from MYRIAD can be found on the project's website at https://myriadproject.org/

[i] Kuyken et al. (2013). Effectiveness of the Mindfulness in Schools Programme: Non-randomised controlled feasibility study. British Journal of Psychiatry, 203(2), 126-131. doi:10.1192/bjp.bp.113.12664
[ii] The Mindfulness Initiative Initial reflections on the MYRIAD study https://www.themindfulnessinitiative.org/myriad-response
[iii] Mindfulness Based Interventions: Teaching Assessment Criteria https://mbitac.bangor.ac.uk/documents/MBITACmanual0517.pdf

CHAPTER 5

How mindfulness works – the mechanisms and the neuroscience

Summary of Chapter 5

This chapter explores the underlying psychological and neuroscientific mechanisms in the mind and brain that can help explain the impacts of mindfulness and its beneficial outcomes for education. It concludes that:

- The structure and function of the brain and nervous system are not fixed in childhood: they remain 'neuroplastic', in other words, changeable, throughout our lives.

- Mindfulness meditation can 'rewire' the brain. It can increases the density and complexity of connections in areas in the brain associated with attention, emotional awareness, self-awareness, introspection, kindness, compassion, and clear thinking. It decreases activity in areas of the brain involved in stress, anxiety, hostility, hyper-vigilance, and impulsivity.

- Mindfulness for teachers and students improves their skills and cultivates attitudes around four psychological core mechanisms: attention, metacognition (standing back from our thought processes), emotion regulation (relating effectively to emotions) and self-regulation (managing our minds).

- Mindfulness meditation reshapes the brain in areas that particularly relate to these mechanisms, although these systems are interrelated and work synergistically.

- All these mechanisms are foundational to the quality of our lives, including the ability of students to learn and flourish, and teachers to be fulfilled and effective.

> **Children are naturally fascinated by the brain. I find that sharing with them what might be happening inside theirs when they practise mindfulness is motivating and increases their curiosity.**

Adrian Bethune, Broughton Junior School

HOW MINDFULNESS WORKS – THE MECHANISMS AND THE NEUROSCIENCE

Why do the psychology and the neuroscience of mindfulness matter?

The application of neuroscience to education, or brain-based learning as it is popularly called, is a growth area of great interest to schools. As a sign of its increasing centrality to education, the medical charity the Wellcome Trust has set up a large-scale public education initiative Understanding Learning: Education and Neuroscience, working closely with the Educational Endowment Fund to disseminate knowledge.[67]

School-based programmes of mindfulness and social and emotional learning increasingly include teaching on brain psychology and neuroscience. Mindfulness in education is a useful pathway to help introduce a basic familiarity and insight into all kinds of neuroscientific mechanisms into the minds of teachers and students.

Psychological and neuroscientific evidence can be highly persuasive to those wondering whether to engage with mindfulness, who often respond well to knowing how and why mindfulness works, rather than just be asked to accept that it does.

The cheering news for educators about neuroplasticity

This whole field is still in its infancy and we need to be careful not to claim too much certainty in an area which, scientists are the first to say, we still barely understand. So what follows here should be seen as promising interim findings.

A basic insight from neuroscience, which is of profound relevance to education, is that the structure and function of the brain and nervous system are not fixed in childhood: these systems remain 'neuroplastic' i.e. changeable throughout our lives.[68] These systems can to some extent be 're-wired' by our behaviours, habits and experiences, including mindfulness meditation, to improve our cognitive and emotional processes and achieve greater

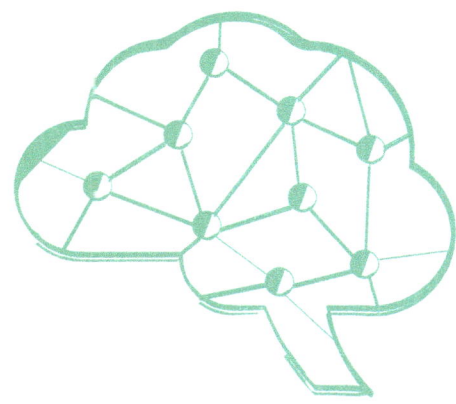

levels of wellbeing, connection with others, health, happiness and personal effectiveness. *'Neurons that fire together wire together'* is a memorable summary of the process. This fundamental insight can be very hopeful and empowering for teachers and students alike.

Mindfulness creates changes in the brain

An increasing number of studies, including brain imaging/MRI (magnetic resonance imaging) studies have explored the impact of mindfulness meditation on brain structures and functions. So far the research has been mainly carried out with adults. They indicate that mindfulness meditation can to an extent 'rewire' the brain to make neural pathways underlying some key abilities and mechanisms more efficient. The cumulative evidence from adult participants, summarised in an influential paper by Tang et al. 'The neuroscience of mindfulness meditation'[69] suggests that meditation can:

- increase the density and complexity of connections in areas associated with beneficial outcomes such as improvements in attention, emotional awareness, self-awareness, introspection, kindness, and compassion.

- decrease activity and growth in those areas involved in anxiety, hostility, hyper-vigilance, impulsivity and the stress response.

> **❝ Due to mindfulness being misunderstood and accessible at the press of a button, it is important for teachers to understand the neuroscience and psychoeducation and exploration that takes place behind it. It is also important for this information to be passed on to parents.**

Springboard Special School, Letchworth Garden City

HOW MINDFULNESS WORKS – THE MECHANISMS AND THE NEUROSCIENCE

A meta-analysis in 2014 by Fox et al. looked at the findings from 21 neuroimaging studies of the brains of about 300 self-described meditators (from many traditions, not just mindfulness).[70] It identified some of the main brain regions that showed a difference in the brains of meditators when compared with an 'average' brain. We list below the regions which showed more activity, density and/or complexity in meditators (except the amygdalae which showed less—see explanation below).

- Anterior cingulate cortex and mid-cingulate cortex: Cortical regions involved in self-regulation, emotion regulation, pain control, attention, self- regulation and self-control and the regulation of the amygdalae.

- Rostrolateral prefrontal cortex: A region associated with meta-awareness (awareness of thinking), introspection, and processing of complex, abstract information.

- Sensory cortices and insular cortex: The main cortical hubs for the processing of tactile information such as touch, pain, conscious proprioception, and body awareness linked to the emotions.

- Superior longitudinal fasciculus and corpus callosum: Subcortical white matter tracts that communicate within and between brain hemispheres.

- Hippocampus: a pair of subcortical structures involved in memory formation and facilitating emotional responses. This area helps to regulate the amygdalae.

- The amygdalae: Two almond-shaped brain structures (one in each hemisphere) that are associated with the processing of emotional stimuli and linking them to learning and memory. The right amygdala is particularly associated with responding to stimuli that are emotionally negative (e.g. threatening). Unlike the other parts of the brain named here, which show more activity and density in meditators, the right amygdala shows less activity and has less grey matter density.

Although the most striking changes to brain structure and function are observable in long-term meditators, the results of MRI scans show that relatively short mindfulness interventions of only eight weeks have some impact.[71]

It's complex

We discuss these mechanisms and the parts of the brain to which they most relate separately, but these are simplified and artificial distinctions to try to make sense of a complex and interconnected process that science itself is only beginning to understand. The psychological mechanisms and the brain, nervous system and body are all interrelated and work synergistically. As Tang et al. remarked, *'The complex mental state of mindfulness is likely to be supported by the large-scale brain networks'*.[72] The whole area is helpfully and clearly summarised in chapter three of Dorjee's *Neuroscience and Psychology of Meditation in Everyday Life*.[73]

Four key mechanisms that mindfulness develops, and the neuroscience that underpins them

We discuss below four interrelated mechanisms around which the emerging research is reasonably solid, and which have clear relevance to education: attention, metacognition, emotion regulation and self-regulation.

Attention

Attention is, psychologically speaking, the behavioural and cognitive process of keeping a focus on a pre-selected object, sensation or other experience, acknowledging but then ignoring any distractions, and returning the focus back to the experience. This process is an ability that can be improved with practice and measured.

> **Attention is sacred because it is the foundation of choice.**
>
> *Tristan Harris, Founder, Center for Humane Technology*

Why does the attention matter to education?

The attention shapes everything about our experience. Attention has been described as our most precious commodity – where we place our attention profoundly shapes the quality of our experience.

- The attention is particularly under threat of 'hijacking' in the modern, fast-paced, digital world. Education needs to help students and staff acquire skills and attitudes to combat potentially toxic levels of distractibility.

- Students cannot learn if they cannot focus and sustain their attention.

- The attention is vital for teacher effectiveness: it underlies the ability to sort priorities, stay on task, and be fully present for the task and for the student.

- For most Westerners, our default attention is often largely on our thoughts. Mindfulness can help us to widen the sphere of what we routinely pay attention to and become more aware of other aspects of our experience. This includes sensations in the body and what is happening in the world around us.

What is the evidence for the impact of mindfulness on attention?

Learning to aim and sustain the attention on a particular aspect of our experience, such as the breath, bodily sensation, a taste, or a sense of movement, is the most fundamental practice in mindfulness meditation, so, unsurprisingly, research evidence shows that the ability is improved by mindfulness practice.

- A recent systematic review by Mak et al. on the impact on attention concluded from seven studies of Mindfulness-Based Interventions (MBIs) with children and young people found that the attention was the area of competence most reliably improved.[74] *'Mindfulness-based interventions are a promising approach to targeting attention …in children and adolescence'.*

- A further systematic review by Dunning et al. of thirty-three MBIs for children and adolescents found significant positive effects on attention.[75]

- In a study of elementary school children, children with poorer ability to manage the attention, particularly those with ADHD, showed the greatest benefit from mindfulness training in terms of improvements in the attention compared with those who started out with higher levels of competence.[76]

- A systematic review of the impacts on the attention of children with ADHD by Tercelli and Ferriera based on ten studies concluded MBIs had 'positive results'[77].

How does mindfulness impact on the parts of the brain particularly involved in the attention?

- Mindfulness practice appears to lead to an increase in activity and increased grey matter changes in the anterior cingulate cortex (ACC).[78] The ACC is a structure located behind the brain's frontal lobe and is the region associated with attention control, and disengaging from and processing distractions.

- Meditators show a greater cortical thickness[79] and greater grey matter concentration in the right anterior insula.[80] As we noted above, sensory cortices and the insular cortex are the main cortical hubs for the processing of tactile information such as touch, pain, conscious proprioception (awareness of the position and movement of the body) and awareness of body sensations. This suggests that the ability to pay attention to sensory experience improves.

Metacognition: standing back from the thought process

Metacognition is a term becoming familiar to educators. The term has many close cousins including meta-cognitive awareness, meta-awareness, meta-cognitive processes, decentering and self-awareness.[81] This set of competences, which for ease we will summarise and oversimplify under the term most familiar to teachers and most often used in the mindfulness literature, metacognition, is at the very heart of mindfulness practice.

This family of related terms refers to various interrelated aspects of the ability to stand back from our experience, including our thoughts and emotions, and examine them more objectively. This process can include examining thoughts and feelings about ourselves: mindfulness can help us decentre and loosen the sense of having a fixed and immutable self at the hub of all things. This can help us embrace a wider perspective in which we take things less personally and are kinder to ourselves and others, recognising our common humanity with other fallible human beings.

Why does metacognition matter to education?

- Metacognition is essential for managing our minds, our lives and our learning. It enables us to think more rationally and realistically, be kinder to ourselves and others, make better choices, to check evidence, and to 'think outside the box' of our own prejudices, habits and views.

- Metacognition is thought to help explain the impact of mindfulness on mental health, enabling sufferers to get more control of the kind of depressive, anxious, judgmental, and ruminative thoughts and the avoidance strategies which can underlie unhelpful responses to distress.[82][83]

HOW MINDFULNESS WORKS – THE MECHANISMS AND THE NEUROSCIENCE

- By enabling us to relate more realistically to our thoughts and feelings, metacognition builds self-compassion, a vital competence for learning. Self-compassion enables us to be more realistic about our failures and setbacks, recognising the inevitable challenges everyone faces. Learners with higher degrees of self-compassion are more effective, as they are likely to be more optimistic and more resilient in the face of difficulties[84]

- Metacognition is a foundational cognitive competence which can underlie all learning, including the ability to reflect, evaluate and think critically. It is one which schools are being encouraged to cultivate. The Education Endowment Foundation has made metacognition (which they define as thinking about thinking) a major focus of recent guidance to schools, connecting it with the competence of self-regulation, which they also see as vital for learning.[85]

What is the evidence for the impact of mindfulness on metacognition?

- A systematic review by Hwang et al. of mindfulness for teachers concluded, from the findings of 13 studies, that mindfulness increases teachers' ability to relate to their experience differently and see it with new eyes (reperceiving). Teachers reported that they found this ability helpful to relieve their stress and be more effective in their work.[86] (We have explored the centrality of such inner shifts for teacher effectiveness in Chapter 3.)

- There is not yet much research on the impact of mindfulness on metacognition in children, however three recent studies investigated this link, including two studies with pre-teens. All three found improvements in metacognition at either post training or follow-up.[87] This is a new and helpful finding for primary education, as doubts have been expressed as to whether younger children are developmentally capable of metacognition.[88]

How does mindfulness impact on the parts of the brain particularly involved in metacognition?

- The neuroscience research to date is with adults, and suggests that mindfulness meditation impacts on the default mode networks, including the anterior cingulate cortex, the ventromedial prefrontal cortex and posterior cingulate cortex, a region associated with both emotion regulation and also meta-awareness (the ability to observe thoughts, feelings, sensations and impulses) introspection, and self-referential processing (reflections on your own identity).[89]

Emotion regulation

Emotion regulation is the process by which we manage our emotions, becoming aware of them, their impacts on mind and body, relating to them effectively, expressing them appropriately, and tracing their roots in the rest of our experience. This competence is profoundly linked in with other mechanisms. How we manage emotions is influenced by our meta-cognitive capacities. We can explore emotions more critically, and see some, such as depressive rumination, as unhelpful passing habits, and others, such as righteous indignation, as pointers for action. Emotion regulation overlaps with attention (there is literally overlap in brain regions activated by both mechanisms). For example, learning to pay closer attention to emotions as they play out in the body can help us become more consciously aware of them, opening the door to responding to them in more effective ways. Mindfulness practice is centrally involved with developing this whole cluster of skills.

Why does emotion regulation matter in education?

- Emotion regulation has been called a 'master competence' which impacts on everything about our lives: our success in school and at work, our relationships, our view of ourselves, and our self-compassion.[90] Schools that help students and staff to improve their emotion regulation skills are likely to be more effective and happier places.

- Copious research has regularly demonstrated that trauma and stress adversely affect the structure, function and effectiveness of the brain and inhibit learning, attention and memory, in both the short and long term.[91]

What is the evidence of the impact of mindfulness on emotion regulation?

- Three recent studies included in a recent systematic review of MBIs for children by Klingbeil et al. (2018) have added to the increasingly convincing evidence base for the impact of MBIs on emotion regulation, including on impulse control, emotional stability, and the ability to show care and respect for oneself and others.[92]

- A recent systematic review of thirteen studies on MBIs for teachers by Emerson et al. (2017)[93] found significant positive effects of MBIs on emotion regulation for 63% of the results of the four studies that measured this.

HOW MINDFULNESS WORKS – THE MECHANISMS AND THE NEUROSCIENCE

How does mindfulness impact on the parts of the brain particularly involved with emotion regulation?

- Emotion regulation takes place right across the brain in a wide range of areas which help us manage our minds.

- The prefrontal cortex is the part of the brain associated with both impulse control and decision making and problem solving. The prefrontal cortex and the anterior cingulate cortex can downregulate the activation in the amygdalae. This appears to be the main pathway for increased emotion regulation in mindfulness in novices, and this part of the brain tends to become more active in the early stages of mindfulness training.[94]

- The hippocampus and the amygdalae, discussed in some detail above, are parts of the limbic system particularly involved in the processing of emotions and memory. The hippocampus, which helps to regulate the activity of the amygdalae, has been found to be more active and denser in meditators. Meanwhile the right amygdala (which particularly responds immediately to perceived threat, sometimes creating an irrational and intense 'emotional hijack' of the brain[95]) is less active and has less grey matter density in regular mediators.

Self-regulation: the master competence

Attention, metacognition and emotion regulation cluster together into the overall 'master' competence of self-regulation.

Self-regulation refers to a cluster of higher-order mental capacities which help us manage our minds, including thoughts, emotions, instincts and actions. These capacities include the ability to monitor, and modify, our thoughts, behaviours, and emotions according to situational demands, to bypass or inhibit impulsive reactions, to overcome distractions, and to persist with tasks we find challenging and unenjoyable. They can also enable us to take effective and ethical action in the face of difficulties and social pressures.

The cumulative impact of mindfulness practice across all of the mechanisms noted above, including the overall domain of self-regulation, can help to explain its foundational effects right across so many educational outcomes.

Why does self-regulation matter to education?

- Self-regulation underlies our ability to be skilful and effective in many areas of our lives: solving problems, planning, organising, making decisions, coping with uncertainty and change and managing our emotions. It enables us to get things done, to manage time, plan, organise, pay attention, and switch focus.[96]

- Evidence suggests a strong relationship between levels of self-regulation and outcomes for people of all ages, including wellbeing, mental health, relationships, and success in life however we choose to define it, while in education it underlies school performance and teacher effectiveness.[97]

What is the evidence for the impact of mindfulness on self-regulation?

- A recent systematic review of thirteen studies on MBIs for teachers by Emerson et al. (2017) concluded that results for self-regulation were particularly strong and it is the area in which mindfulness for teachers 'showed strongest promise'.[98] Qualitative work included in the review showed that teachers regularly report that it is the aspect of MBIs they find most helpful in managing their stress, in avoiding self-blame, and teaching effectively.

- A recent systematic review by Dunning et al. (2018) of 33 studies including 3,666 children and adolescents, found significant positive effects of MBIs on self-regulation.[99]

How does mindfulness impact on the parts of the brain particularly involved in self-regulation?

- All of the areas of the brain mentioned above contribute to the master competence of self-regulation.

- More specifically, mindfulness meditators showed more activity and grey matter in parts of the brain such as the anterior cingulate cortex and mid-cingulate cortex, cortical regions involved in self-regulation, emotion regulation, pain control, attention, and self-control.[100][101]

HOW MINDFULNESS WORKS – THE MECHANISMS AND THE NEUROSCIENCE

A model for how mindfulness, the mechanisms it cultivates, and its outcomes are related

Mindfulness
Chapter 1

- Means intentionally paying attention to present-moment experience
- Cultivates attitude of openness, curiosity, kindness and care
- Cultivates new relationship with experience - 'moving towards'
- Cultivates joy, compassion, wisdom, equanimity
- Sustained, intensive training in mindfulness meditation and embodied practice
- Supported by experiential enquiry-based learning process
- Taught by teacher with competence in mindfulness plus grasp of the context and needs of the students

mechanisms
Chapter 5

- Attention
- Metacognition
- Emotional Regulation
- Self-regulation

Outcomes
Chapters 2, 3 and 4

Teachers
- Improved psycho-social and physical wellbeing
- Reduction in mental health problems – stress, depression, anxiety, burnout
- Greater teacher effectiveness – prioritising, focus, on task, teaching child not just subject
- Compassion to self and others, attunement, presence

Children and young people
- Improved psycho-social and physical wellbeing
- Reduced mental health problems – stress, anxiety, depression
- Improved social and emotional skills
- Improved behaviour
- Improved cognition and learning
- Improved academic performance

> ❝ I saw my kids stopping and going. 'OK I'm stuck on a problem but actually I'm not going to beat myself up about it, I'm just going to take a minute, I'm going to focus on my breathing, I'm going to relax and then I'm going to come back to it.'

Secondary teacher.

PART THREE

IMPLEMENTING MINDFULNESS IN SCHOOLS

CHAPTER 6

Establishing the foundations

Summary of Chapter 6

This chapter outlines the initial foundations the evidence suggests need to be in place if mindfulness is to flourish and be sustained. The following appear to be vital:

- Starting where schools are and integrating mindfulness with educational language and thinking.

- Matching the evidence of the impact of mindfulness to the school's priorities and needs, while clarifying that mindfulness is a long-term process, not a quick fix.

- Establishing effective champions to catalyse and lead the process.

- Engaging the Senior Leadership Team, ideally as practitioners not just supporters.

- Ensuring widespread understanding of mindfulness across the whole staff.

- Using inspirational first-hand experience and testimonials.

- Allocating sufficient resources such as timetabling and finance.

> My top suggestion? Do your research then put together a proposal for mindfulness to the Headteacher and SLT. Writing a formal proposal and highlighting the wellbeing benefits to staff and students will help. Try to link the proposal to the Ofsted framework, School Development Plan (SDP) and curriculum offer. Including costings and potential savings is helpful. Sell them the idea of why you believe mindfulness would have a positive impact on our young people.

Dacorum Education Support Centre, Hertfordshire

Integrating mindfulness with educational language and thinking

Modern mindfulness is still finding its feet in educational contexts, having developed mostly in the world of healthcare. It helps mindfulness teaching to integrate more easily into schools at the outset of the journey if it is not presented as too 'left field', 'therapeutic' or 'medical' but is framed in educational thinking, aims and language, fitting in with current policy and practice.

In terms of the implementation of innovations, some schools may be turning to guidance on school improvement from bodies such as the respected Education Endowment Foundation (EEF), whose useful summary diagram of the implementation and evaluation process is outlined below. This guidance over the first three of our chapters on implementation is broadly aligned with the EEF framework. In later stages this guidance goes beyond it to consider how mindfulness can move on from being a discrete intervention to also becoming a way of being, embedded within the broader processes and ethos of schools, classrooms and staffrooms.

Matching mindfulness to the school's priorities and needs

If it is to catch fire, any meaningful educational innovation in a school needs to start with what matters to the many stakeholders involved and their felt needs.

A school may already have a clear sense of its priorities through regular processes of self-reflection and audit.

These can be matched with the evidence base for mindfulness (outlined in part two) to align the school's priorities to what mindfulness might realistically achieve.

It is important to manage expectations and to clarify that implementation is a long-term, slow burn: it can take a number of years to establish across a school setting and build capacity.

Putting evidence to work: A school's guide to implementation

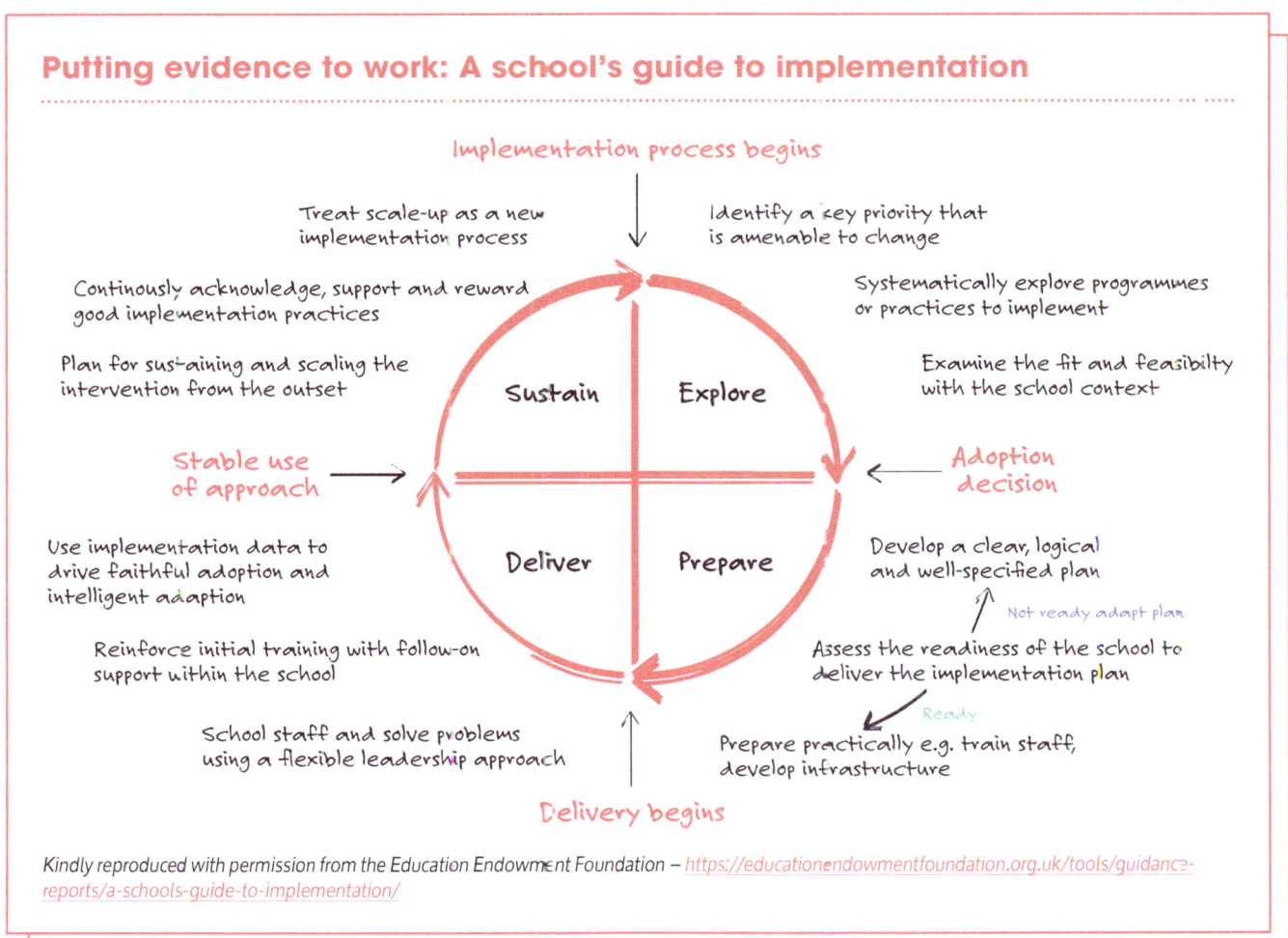

Kindly reproduced with permission from the Education Endowment Foundation – https://educationendowmentfoundation.org.uk/tools/guidance-reports/a-schools-guide-to-implementation/

ESTABLISHING THE FOUNDATIONS

Establishing effective champions

A study by Wilde et al. on the implementation of a UK school programme, found that champions are needed at the outset to catalyse the introduction of mindfulness, advocate for it, and steer the process.[102] The study found that without enthusiasm and strong leadership from the outset, mindfulness faltered. High staff turnover and one or more key people leaving were shown in a study by Mendelson et al. to be a frequent cause of a mindfulness programme stalling or failing.[103] Some schools start by establishing a 'mindfulness lead' to get things moving; however for mindfulness to thrive and be sustained, single champions need to grow quickly into a strong team, and mindfulness needs to be firmly established in the school improvement and development plan.

Engaging the Senior Leadership Team (SLT)

Strong, informed and committed leadership is essential to all school improvement, including mindfulness. Research by Hudson et al. on the factors that influence the take up of mindfulness in schools suggests energetic leadership from an engaged SLT is the single most essential feature in determining the quality of a mindfulness programme and whether it is sustained.[104]

Members of the SLT need to understand mindfulness, believe that it contributes centrally to the school's core mission and values and communicate this conviction robustly and consistently to their staff, students and parents. It helps to 'hit the buttons' that matter to the SLT, which are often practical issues around finance, evidence, outcomes and accountability.

> **LEARNING FROM PROFESSIONAL PRACTICE**
>
> ### A primary schools starts with a concern for mental health and ends by developing a new school ethos
>
> In 2017, school leaders became aware of increasing concern around pupils exhibiting difficulties with social, emotional and mental health needs and these issues were being seen both within the playground and within the learning in lessons…Led by the head teacher, the school began looking into wellbeing and mindfulness, through practices such as yoga and meditation, as well as mindfulness and reflection in lessons, so children were able to reflect and pause on their learning and attitudes. This led to a new culture being developed where mental health and wellbeing was valued alongside academic achievements. The school planned strategic actions to embed mindfulness and wellbeing across the school culture and started with staff training to ensure staff bought into the new ethos and supported it.
>
> *Eyres Monsell Primary School, Leicester*

> **KEY ISSUE**
> ### What makes an effective mindfulness champion?
>
> - They have a clear understanding of what mindfulness is and is not.
>
> - They have a realistic grasp of the evidence base, to help them to tailor mindfulness to the needs of the school and its members, but not to overpromise.
>
> - They have a committed and regular personal mindfulness practice.
>
> - They are far enough up the hierarchy and with enough 'clout' to make things happen.
>
> - They are skilled communicators and organisers, capable of motivating others.
>
> - They are resourceful, flexible, open-minded and create connections and seize opportunities.
>
> - They are patient and take the long view, being aware that mindfulness cannot be developed quickly: the vital ingredient of staff ownership and engagement cannot be hurried.

> **Get the staff to buy in first; if they are going to be leading it, they need to believe in it!**
>
> *Abertillery Learning Community, Blaenau Gwent*

As any web search will show, there is a thriving knowledge base developing on leadership for mindfulness in organisations. A specific literature and evidence base is now starting to develop on mindful school leadership.[105] One of the key findings of this whole literature is that it helps greatly in sustaining and embedding mindfulness if the SLT are at the heart of the process, lead the team of champions, and themselves walk the talk, embody and practice mindfulness and integrate it into their own lives and leadership, rather than just cheering from the sidelines.

Spreading understanding across the school community

Although it is not realistic to expect that all school staff will be drawn to practise mindfulness themselves, let alone teach it to students, it is helpful to have sound school-wide understanding of what mindfulness is and is not, and widespread support for its introduction. The audience needs to include administrative and support staff, who research shows are highly influential.[106]

A frequently used method to convey a basic understanding of mindfulness is an introductory/taster session, offered to all staff and possibly extended to governors and parents. Students may need their own version. This will outline the theory and the evidence, give some brief experience of practice and an outline of the next steps.

LEARNING FROM PROFESSIONAL PRACTICE

Mindfulness course for school leaders helps with stress and overwhelm

The Reach2 Academy Trust is the largest primary-only academy trust, supporting about 60 primary schools across England. Between September 2018 and June 2019, 24 senior leaders within the trust completed the mindfulness programme 'To Be and to Lead'.

School leaders followed a three-day residential course that taught both core mindfulness skills and attitudes plus a focus on enriching and sustaining ourselves as leaders, with joy, gratitude and appreciation. Practice between residentials was supported by regular emails and buddy groups.

The programme was externally evaluated by the University of Sunderland, using anonymous pre and post questionnaires. Improvements were found on all indicators: particularly strong positive outcomes included:

- Having a good night's sleep whatever the pressure and work-life balance: both increased by over 50%.

- Being hard on themselves when not living up to their expectations, feeling overwhelmed by work and running on autopilot, all decreased by 30% or more.

- Managing high pressure, noticing times of satisfaction at work and dealing skillfully with challenging colleagues when under pressure all showed increases of between 25% and 30%.

Catherine Paine, Deputy Chief Executive, Reach2 Academy Trust, Burton Upon Trent

---

> **We introduced mindfulness largely through the Mind UP curriculum which was introduced and initially led as a project by the Headteacher working with a parent governor who had an interest in mindfulness in schools. As senior leaders were engaged from the start, support and innovation was quickly established.**
>
> *West Rise Community interest school, East Sussex*

ESTABLISHING THE FOUNDATIONS

Using inspirational first-hand experience and testimonials

Most people respond best to stories; summaries of numerical evidence are often not as powerful as first-hand experience. Mindfulness in schools is usually catalysed initially by the personal experience of an adult, ideally the headteacher, if not a teacher or senior manager, who had found it helpful for themselves and who can communicate their convincing enthusiasm.

Staff and student testimonials can be uniquely powerful in persuading stakeholders of the value of mindfulness. In Chapter 10 on evaluation we encourage you to collect your own inspirational quotes and stories from your school community.

> **When introducing mindfulness to a multi-academy trust my experience suggests a top-down meets bottom-up approach. This might involve securing trust and senior leader support whilst building up a coalition of positive staff and pupils at individual school level.**
>
> Amanda Bailey, Star Academies

LEARNING FROM PROFESSIONAL PRACTICE

A primary school uses its additional funding for mindfulness

Lynburn Primary School is a state school located in an area of Dunfermline which is comprised predominately of social/council owned housing. A significant number of the children are impacted by poverty, drug and alcohol addiction and other family difficulties. As a result, the school is in receipt of PEF (Pupil Equity Funding). The headteacher has used much of this additional funding to support the children's emotional wellbeing and mental health. Some of this funding has been allocated to introduce mindfulness to the school community.

Lynburn Primary School, Fife

Allocating sufficient resources

The allocation of sufficient resources is vital. It includes time for staff development, time in the curriculum and on the timetable, sufficient administrative support, and sufficient funding for quality training and ongoing support for staff, all of which have been shown to be essential. With schools under many competing pressures for time and money, lack of resources is one of the most common barriers to implementing mindfulness. Linking mindfulness with pupil priorities, as Lynburn Primary has done, may help to tap into funding streams.

 EXPLORE FURTHER
Where to find some inspirational video clips

The inputs of the speakers at the Mindfulness in Schools Project (MiSP) conferences include teachers and young people as well as experts and may provide inspirational clips. The 2020 conference can be found here: https://mindfulnessinschools.org/teaching-mindfully-videos/

There are talking-head videos of school children and teachers, sharing the impacts of mindfulness on the websites of MiSP and the Youth Mindfulness Project.

- https://virtual-institute.youthmindfulness.org/courses/youth-mindfulness-kids-programme-teacher-training

- https://mindfulnessinschools.org/videos/

CHAPTER 7

Developing mindfulness for teachers

Summary of Chapter 7

This chapter explores the issues around mindfulness for the teachers themselves. It is illustrated with school-based examples. The evidence and practice suggest that:

- Mindfulness in schools needs to begin with the teachers themselves, so they can experience personal benefits, understand mindfulness fully, use mindfulness to become more effective classroom teachers and act as credible, embodied teachers of mindfulness for students.

- There are various models and approaches to teacher development and preparation, from eight-week foundation courses, through in-house teaching by programmes, through to teachers and students learning together.

- In the face of financial pressures and the wish to roll out mindfulness quickly, we need to gather robust evidence on what types of teacher preparation lead to what outcomes.

- Staff will need ongoing support and staff development to deepen their motivation, understanding and practice.

> **❝❝ Develop your own mindfulness practice initially – young people can sense if you don't practise what you preach.**
>
> Clare Winter, SENDCo at DESC - a pupil referral unit, Hertfordshire

DEVELOPING MINDFULNESS FOR TEACHERS

Why do we need to start with the teachers?

Good teachers are at the heart of any effective classroom, and any good school, and mindful teachers are at the heart of mindfulness in schools. Chapter 3 outlines in detail the increasingly robust evidence for the impact of mindfulness on staff wellbeing and staff effectiveness. This cumulative evidence suggests that there are strong reasons for the development of mindfulness skills, attitudes and capacities to begin with teachers and other adults in schools, indicating that:

- Teachers with greater levels of wellbeing and lower stress are more resilient and effective teachers.

- Mindfulness helps teachers, whatever their subject, to become more reflective teachers, and more skilful and effective in their core job of managing their classrooms, delivering impactful teaching and learning, and relating positively to their students.

- Mindfulness enables teachers to create effective, reflective, connected classroom climates.

- As Chapter 1 made clear, mindfulness is not just a curriculum, nor even just a set of skills: it is a way of being. Teachers need to learn mindfulness themselves and practise it regularly in their own lives if they are to be embodied, present and credible teachers of mindfulness. Mindfulness has to be experienced from the inside to be properly understood. A familiar analogy is with water and swimming. You would not want your child taught to swim by someone who had never entered water and had only a theoretical understanding of it.

Ensuring teachers work with a full model of mindfulness

The paper discussed in Chapter 1 on 'the warp and the weft' presents a consensus on what mindfulness means and outlines the qualities needed in any mindfulness teacher.[107] The basic requirements are that they need to possess:

- the competences to teach mindfulness, including a clear understanding of what mindfulness is and how it works.

- the embodied qualities and attitudes core to mindfulness, such as kindness, non-judgementalism, curiosity, presence, and present-moment awareness.

- a committed ongoing mindfulness practice of an appropriate kind, including in everyday life.

The extent to which this is currently being fully achieved is doubtful. A review by Emerson et al. of the quality of the teaching of mindfulness in schools suggested quality was generally not high, with few teachers following the programme instructions fully, and three-quarters of teachers delivering mindfulness in schools not being trained to recognised standards.[108] A small-scale study by Wiglesworth and Quinn also paints a picture of teachers' variable understanding, with most of them seeing mindfulness as calm and relaxation, missing a vital aspect, which is that mindfulness is about relating to difficult experience in a new way.[109] There is clearly a need to support teachers to follow programme protocols fully, and work with a full model of mindfulness, both so they can benefit from it for themselves and as a solid foundation to teach others.

LEARNING FROM PROFESSIONAL PRACTICE
Mindfulness improves wellbeing and the leadership abilities of senior school leaders in Wales

In some parts of Wales where mindfulness is being developed at a national level as part of a new Curriculum for Wellbeing the process is beginning with wellbeing of school leaders.

As part of the Innovation Pathway of the National Academy for Education Leadership in Wales, the Mindfulness for Education Leaders course has been established for heads and senior leaders in education in Wales. Overwhelmingly, participants have commented on the improvement in their self-awareness and levels of self-care, with many holding these to be fundamental foundations of other leadership behaviours such as decision-making and relationship building. There is an appetite to take mindfulness back to their settings and develop strategies for staff and pupil wellbeing.

Liz Williams, Co-lead with the Welsh Government for developing a Mindfulness Toolkit for Wales and Chair of Mindfulness Wales

> **RESEARCH EVIDENCE**
> ## Teachers sometimes fail fully to understand mindfulness
>
> Interviews with a cross section of ten teachers of mindfulness in schools in the north of England found they generally had a poor, and sometimes completely wrong, understanding of what mindfulness is.
>
> **Almost all (ten) teachers understood mindfulness as an awareness of one's emotions or thoughts,** though few mentioned this awareness should be focused in the present moment and be non-judgmental. Only one teacher associated mindfulness practice with an acceptance of one's emotions: **'[knowing] it's actually okay to be flustered or stressed'** ...two teachers appeared to associate mindfulness more with a sense of mindlessness or a method of distraction... **these teachers referred to 'emptying your thoughts' or 'taking your mind off things'.**
>
> Wigelsworth, M. and Quinn, A. (2020): Mindfulness in schools: an exploration of teachers' perceptions of mindfulness-based interventions, Pastoral Care in Education, DOI: 10.1080/02643944.2020.1725908

Routes into training to teach mindfulness

Quality foundational training for the teachers themselves takes time, money and commitment, but schools that have succeeded in implementing mindfulness generally report that it is well worth the initial investment.

Undertaking an eight-week course

The safest and most evidence-based route for teachers to begin the journey with a full understanding of mindfulness is to start by experiencing for themselves as participants a good-quality mindfulness programme, aimed at cultivating their own wellbeing, taught by a teacher fully trained in that programme.

A safe starting point is an eight-week course for adults, such as Mindfulness-Based Stress Reduction and Mindfulness-Based Cognitive Therapy courses taught by a BAMBA recognised teacher.

Many school-based programmes and initiatives strongly recommend that those who wish to train with them first follow this tried and tested route to provide a solid basis for the specific training they offer. The current Wellbeing Curriculum in Wales, which is including mindfulness as an essential component, is sending as many staff as possible on an eight-week course, which it reports minimises the costs of extra training thereafter.[110]

The British Association for Mindfulness-Based Approaches holds a list of facilitators who have trained and qualified to teach these eight-week courses through a recognised route and who follow their Good Practice Guidelines. https://bamba.org.uk/

Foundation courses run by mindfulness in schools programmes

Some programmes, such as the Mindfulness in Schools Project ('MiSP') cluster of courses, and The Present, provide their own foundational courses to cultivate mindfulness for the teacher themselves, plus then further training to learn how to teach a course to students. This approach may work well with time-stressed teachers and has the advantage of overlap in the style and content between the adult and the student versions of the courses. The MiSP .b Foundations course, a eight-week course for the teachers themselves, has been evaluated in a small control trial, and showed significant impacts on teacher wellbeing, stress and depression.[111]

Some providers, such as MiSP and The Present, also offer courses for suitably qualified people to then go on to train others to teach these foundational courses. (See the table of programmes in Appendix 1 for details on which programmes offer what levels of training).

> ❝ **Be prepared to start small and grow slowly investing in mindfulness teacher training as you go to ensure sustainability over the long term.**
>
> Amanda Bailey, Star Academies

Face to face or online?

Attending a face-to-face course is probably ideal, but often difficult, especially where budgets are tight and in widely spread rural locations. The COVID-19 pandemic has, at the time of writing, made it impossible, and has required many training providers to move firmly into the online world. There are some well-designed online foundational courses now available, and we have links to some of them in Appendix 4, useful websites. This online trend looks set to continue after the pandemic and has the potential advantage of making mindfulness training more accessible and sustainable, although the quality of such training in comparison with face to face would need to be evaluated.

Teachers and students learn together

A 'teach yourself' approach is one which provides instructions and materials with which teachers new to mindfulness can engage their students in an experience of mindfulness practice and exercises at the same time as learning it themselves.

Some step-by-step self-help classroom instruction manuals that can be bought off the shelf stand out from the others in having been written by experts and describing how to apply evidence-based programmes previously tested in published trials.[112]

> **Mindfulness has allowed me to be more present for my students, my family and my faith. It has enabled me to become more resilient with the challenges I face at work and in seeing the effectiveness of the practice I have been motivated to share this with others.**

Nafisah – Teacher, Eden Girls' Leadership Academy, Slough

> **We are five years into our journey at DESC and initially, many of the staff were resistant. Now some staff have signed up to the .b Foundations course and have even made it an appraisal target.**

Dacorum Education Support Centre, A Pupil Referral Unit, Hertfordshire

Teachers and students learning together is an approach embraced in the UK by Jigsaw, the mindful approach to PSHE, which includes elements of mindfulness practice within a broader PSHE curriculum, an increasingly popular link that we explore in Chapter 8. They also offer optional support from an online community and team of PSHE consultants. Case study qualitative 'success stories' and an as yet unpublished evaluation suggests it is on the whole popular with students and teachers, although it is not possible to separate out the mindfulness element within the wider PSHE curriculum.

There are so far no published trials to indicate the extent to which teachers new to mindfulness learning alongside students, or working from teach-yourself manuals, can achieve the outcomes shown in Chapter 2 (where teachers are trained first).

The need for more data

In the face of financial pressures and the wish to roll out mindfulness quickly, we need to gather robust evidence on what types of teacher preparation lead to what outcomes, what is a 'good enough' and cost-effective approach and what is too diluted to make any measurable difference. Recent research evaluating the effectiveness of different types and intensity of teacher training course suggests that all kinds of preparation are not in fact yet leading to teachers in schools having sufficient skills to teach mindfulness as effectively as they need to, and that we need to both look more to the quality of training and to provide more ongoing support for trained teachers.[113]

Giving ongoing support and professional development

It is not surprising that the research cited above suggests that the various forms of teacher preparation are just the start in developing a skilled teacher who can sustain mindfulness in their classroom and school. Teaching skills are deepened through practice. So there is clearly a need for trained teachers to receive ongoing support and professional development to improve their competences. Time is precious in hard-pressed schools, but many are finding it time and cost effective, as well as helpful for wellbeing, to support staff to sustain and deepen their experience of mindfulness and encouraging and normalising practice, in optional ways of course. Some tried and tested methods include:

- offering lunchtime drop-in sit groups (some schools open these up to students).

- offering online weekly sit groups (some were set up during the pandemic and proved useful).

- forming pairs or small groups of practice buddies.

- paying for staff use of apps.

- integrating short grounding practices routinely in staff meetings, to help people take a moment and return to themselves and be fully present at the start and finish, or during heated or difficult discussions.

- allowing time and financial support to attend further mindfulness courses, conferences and retreats to deepen staff knowledge, practice, skills and confidence, and offering professional development.

- giving staff the opportunity to attend mindfulness leadership training so they can support their team to develop their understanding, skills and practice.

Supportive networks of schools

It is often convincing for a school to see an intervention or approach work well for others. In some areas, schools are linking together to share inspirational good practice.

> **Mindfulness had been drip fed gently throughout the whole school these last few years, and we have embedded the values of mindfulness with all pupils and staff. Other schools now visit us to observe our practice.**

Debbie Cass, Dell Primary School, Monmouthshire

CHAPTER 8

Teaching mindfulness to students

Summary of Chapter 8

This chapter explores the issues that need to be considered when introducing mindfulness to students. The evidence and good practice suggest that:

- teachers developing their own approaches can work if the teacher has a solid background in mindfulness, a personal practice, and is a skilled classroom teacher.

- using an established programme is a more reliable option for most schools: the programme needs to be selected for fit and feasibility in the school.

- sticking to the programme as written in the first instance is important. If a tailored approach is needed, use that at the outset.

- using an 'inside' teacher is the most effective approach but only if they have an established understanding and practice. If not, an 'outside' facilitator can be effective, although this may not lead to embedding mindfulness in the school. Partnerships between both can work well.

- mindfulness teaching needs to be based on warm and trusting relationships between teacher and student.

- methods need to be lively and engaging, and with the teacher using their usual skilful classroom management practices to set boundaries and help students learn.

- reflective enquiry following practice, which helps students focus on their immediate experience in mind and body, is vital, and often hard for teachers, who tend to be used to helping people move to abstractions and to find answers.

- students who do more practice outside class tend to show more benefit, so it helps to find invitational ways to encourage this.

- peer learning can be empowering.

- mindfulness meditation is not for everyone: it needs to be invitational, and care needs to be taken to safeguard students and their vulnerabilities.

Choosing the approach

The teacher creates their own approach

Experienced classroom teachers who are familiar with mindfulness and have a personal practice may feel they can create appropriate ways to teach mindfulness practice to their students. They may feel they have the critical and professional ability to use their own experience to follow first principles. If so they have a wealth of published resources, books, manuals, curricula and lesson plans, apps and animations that can be bought off the shelf from which to choose those best suited to their classes. This approach is likely to be easier for the early years and primary school class teacher, who can fit in regular short practices, integrated into the daily routines of teaching their class.

We list some key readings, websites and apps in Appendices 3 and 4.

Creating bespoke materials and resources, perhaps in addition to a core programme, may well be essential where the approach needs to be closely tailored to the needs of students, such as those with Special Educational Needs and Disabilities (SEND), those with high levels of disadvantage, or from minority cultures. We discuss how mindfulness can meet the needs of a wider range of students further below.

Choosing an established programme: exploring fit and feasibility

There may be clear reasons to adopt an existing programme. For instance:

- To seek the confidence of knowing your school is building on the expertise of others with a sound reputation.

- Where a programme clearly fits your school context well.

- To have the ongoing support of an established programme and the community of teachers it has created.

Appendix 1 is a table of the main providers and programmes currently running in the UK. The characteristics of the programmes listed there may help to guide your school to a provider and programme that is suitable for your context, staff, students, style, values and level of resources.

Programme fidelity or adaptation?

A great deal of thought and testing will probably have gone into the design of any published programme you choose, so if you have chosen one you think fits your context, and with an attendant investment of your time and money, it makes sense to give the programme a proper trial and run it as written, at least to begin with (which is adhering to so-called 'programme fidelity'). This will include following the curriculum and structure, a script if there is one, and teaching it only to the group for whom it is intended, before you consider any major adaptations of content or extensions to other groups.

Programme fidelity is generally considered to be essential to the successful implementation and subsequent impact of any programme.[114] Teachers can find this difficult to do: an analysis by Emerson et al. in 2020 of the quality of the teaching of mindfulness in schools found few teachers following the programme instructions fully.[115] Where programme fidelity is not followed the research is clear that social-emotional learning interventions in general, and mindfulness in particular, are less likely to show impact.[116]

There may be good reasons why you need to adapt from the outset, and if you judge that you need a programme or approach to be adaptable, perhaps because your students are diverse and with particular needs and challenges, it is best to pick a programme that is more principles-driven, and is designed to be tailored.

> **At Youth Mindfulness we found we needed to adapt our lessons and course aims to each group we worked with, as each group had different dispositions, needs and aspirations. For this reason, we started to adopt a flexible and responsive approach, tailoring our lessons to each group.**

Michael Bready, founder and director, Youth Mindfulness

TEACHING MINDFULNESS TO STUDENTS

Using an internal or external teacher of mindfulness?

The 'warp and weft' paper cited in Chapter 1, on establishing benchmarks for the quality of mindfulness teaching, suggested that, in addition to having sufficient expertise in mindfulness, teachers of mindfulness also need to be at home in the context in which the course is to be taught, and be:

- trained to teach the particular programme being offered.

- an expert in the particular target group, with specialist knowledge, experience and professional training related to the population they are teaching - in this case, teachers and school students.[117]

A recent meta-analysis of research looking at the quality and impact of various ways of delivering mindfulness programmes in schools by Carsley et al. shows that programmes taught to students are most effective when they are delivered by members of the school community such as a teacher, counsellor or mentor.[118] However, 'inside' teachers are only more effective than outsiders if they understand mindfulness fully and have a solid mindfulness practice.

Carsley et al.'s analysis suggested that the next most effective approach after utilising a skilled and knowledgeable member of the school staff, is to appoint an outside facilitator with deep expertise of authentic mindfulness. Their continuing involvement and befriending of the programme can help keep a school on track. However, employing an outsider is only a starting point, and is not in itself likely to lead to the longer-term embedding and sustaining of mindfulness across the school, nor do much to develop the vital foundation of staff mindfulness. Those not trained to teach in schools and not familiar with individual students may take time to learn the classroom management skills of engaging 30 lively youngsters.

Some schools have found that forming co-teaching partnerships between mindfulness experts and skilled and experienced classroom teachers can be the best of both worlds.

> **We found that before any significant learning could take place, the young people needed to feel safe, and the most powerful way to help a group of young people feel safe to engage and explore mindfulness was by focusing on building positive relationships**
>
> *Michael Bready, founder and director, Youth Mindfulness*

LEARNING FROM PROFESSIONAL PRACTICE

An outside facilitator describes the pros and cons of her role

As an external deliverer with my own practice and values I felt that I could connect well with the children over the six weeks, though the greater impact on the children and staff would be felt in embedding the learning and practices between the lessons and after I had left, making sure the teachers were fully engaged. The challenge in my role has been to develop the teachers' value and understanding of practice and the learning from the lessons so that it becomes a lifelong skill. With teachers being so busy, the temptation is for them to mark books while I teach, however their presence during the lessons is just as important as mine.

From a case study written by an outsider facilitator working with 10 schools. https://mindfulnessinschools.org/wp-content/uploads/2020/07/Case-Study-Seth-Foster.pdf)

> **It is important never to force participation as mindfulness isn't for everyone. Gentle encouragement and kindness and an awareness of how individual pupils feel is key.**
>
> *Culcross Primary School, Fife*

TEACHING MINDFULNESS TO STUDENTS

MOVING INTO THE CLASSROOM

Mindfulness teaching is founded on relationships

Effective mindfulness teaching is based primarily on sound, warm, honest and trusting relationships between teachers and students. The qualities of the teacher, including their ability to build warm relationships with students and help them feel safe [119], are key determinants of the success of all teaching and learning. These qualities are absolutely essential in social and emotional areas such as mindfulness, where the agenda is not the imparting of outside knowledge but the development of the inner person.

Mindfulness cannot be coercive: the tone needs to be gentle and invitational. Students need to know that these sessions are 'for them' as opposed to being part of a broader assessment framework.

Engaging teaching and learning methods

Providing engaging ways to teach mindfulness in age-appropriate ways to young people is a core feature of well-designed programmes.

Teachers who have learned mindfulness for their own wellbeing will not find the pace and style of teaching used in adult classes transfer to school classrooms all that easily. Teachers need to free their minds and imaginations to use all the lively, creative, imaginative and age-appropriate techniques at their disposal to keep the young audience engaged, while staying true to the aims of mindfulness. Mindfulness needs to be experienced by the students as easy, fun, lively, clearly relevant to themselves and the circumstances, and useful right from the outset, if 'conscript' audiences are to stay with it. Teachers also need to remember to use their classroom management skills to set boundaries, keep order and allow everyone to learn: children do not become saints or monks just because we are teaching them mindfulness.

> **LEARNING FROM PROFESSIONAL PRACTICE**
>
> **Using lively methods for 'at risk' students:**
>
> Students in small groups learn mindfulness through expressive arts, yoga, and mindful hip hop. Through this program, we target the most "at-risk" students and pair them with high-achieving students to encourage cohesive non-judgmental teams and community. Sessions are 45-minutes long, and students are referred to the program by principals, teachers and support staff. This year, we served 660 students at 19 out of 22 underserved schools through Rise-Up.
>
> *From the 2020 annual report of the Mindful Life project.*
> http://mindfullifeproject.org/ourwork2b/

> **TOOL BOX**
> **Three basic principles for guiding practices with children and young people**
>
> - The teacher will need a balance between being in the moment mentally and physically themselves and staying alert in 'classroom management' mode, especially while the class settles to the idea of practice.
>
> - Using the present participle 'ing' rather than the imperative (e.g. 'breathing in' rather than 'breathe in') brings a soft and invitational quality.
>
> - Talking impersonally e.g., about 'the body' and 'thoughts' rather than 'your body' or 'your thoughts', encourages decentering and a sense of sharing a common experience.

> **❝ I could see the benefits quickly as students warmed to the easy mindful techniques of FOFBOC (feet on floor, bottom on chair) and 7/11 (relaxation breathing) and were receptive to the excellent teaching materials with easy watchable animations.**
>
> Jo Price, University of Kent Academies Trust Talking about the Mindfulness in Schools Project .b programme

The Mindfulness Initiative / Implementing Mindfulness in Schools

TEACHING MINDFULNESS TO STUDENTS

The physical space will probably be a normal cluttered classroom, not particularly quiet or meditative. This is in fact helpful, as it is in the midst of ordinary life that we all need to learn to be fully present. If the classroom set-up is a horseshoe of chairs, turning the chairs out during practices can encourage students not to disturb one another. Routines such as undoing ties or taking shoes off and sounding a chime or bell (if there are no concerns about religious connotations) can help the class transition and settle.

In primary classrooms with one teacher and one class for a length of time, mindfulness practices may be very short and spread out, integrated into the day. It is likely to be delivered as a discrete whole-period lesson in a secondary school or college, with more substantial periods of practice and time for reflection.

The central role of reflective enquiry

When following a mindfulness foundation course for themselves, teachers will have experienced skilfully led periods of reflection after the meditation and other types of mindfulness practice, often called 'enquiry' in this context. Similar periods of what we might call 'reflection' in a school context are an equally important part of teaching mindfulness to the young, especially to older students.

As with all experiential learning, reflective enquiry is a part of an action, reflection, learning, re-application cycle. Reflection helps learners to focus on the salient parts of the real-life experience they just had, be clearer about the point of the practice and what they might take from it, be able to generalise from this specific instance, and anticipate applying their learning in real-life situations.[120]

Anecdotal evidence suggests that teachers often find getting the open-minded tone for reflective enquiry tricky; it can easily slip into didactic instruction, and into 'fixing' problems. In contrast, a mindful reflection/enquiry:

- Uses open-ended questions to help students become more sensitive to their immediate experience in the here and now, and in a non-judgmental way.

- Encourages all responses evenly, being equally comfortable with 'boring' and 'don't know' as with 'calming' and 'lovely'.

- Gently steers discussion away from theorising and digressions and back to the here and now.

- Meets and gently dispels familiar misconceptions about 'clearing the mind', 'stopping thinking' and 'feeling better', judgments which are followed almost inevitably by, 'So, I'm no good at it'.

- Focuses instead on the lived experience there in the classroom, and on what is actually happening in mind, body and senses.

Leading this kind of open-minded reflective enquiry can be a transformative experience for the teacher themselves, helping them to internalise more thoroughly how mindfulness is essentially about relating to our experience in a new way, not immediately 'fixing things' for ourselves or others, or moving to theory and abstraction.

Reflective enquiry is also essential to help students be aware of the inner personal skills relating to vital underlying mechanisms they are developing through their experience, such as self-regulation, kindness and compassion, and metacognition. This will in turn help them to link what they are learning in mindfulness classes with parallel work in the mainstream curriculum on the process of learning, focusing on developing their skills of paying attention, metacognition (standing back from the thought process), critical thinking, and open-mindedness. We explore what value mindfulness can add to the process of learning in the mainstream curriculum later in this chapter.

> **Pupils often say 'it was boring' to which I ask, 'Aah boring – when did you notice that and how do you know you were bored?' This can be quite a revelation to pupils who may be used to being chastised for suggesting a lesson is boring and encourages them to reflect and notice what boredom feels like.**

Amanda Bailey, Star Academies

TEACHING MINDFULNESS TO STUDENTS

> **The children used the practices to help them in many different ways…to help with friends and family, to cope with difficult feelings, to help with performance in sport, drama and music, and to support themselves when 'having a wobble'.**

Mark Penney, Solihull Junior School

Encouraging practice outside class

The amount of informal practice your students undertake outside class is likely to be a strong determinant on how impactful mindfulness teaching in class is, and whether it is sustained after the lessons are over.[121] Some practical strategies that have been found gently to encourage informal practice include the following:

- Avoid the word 'homework' – even 'home practice' can hit the wrong button. 'Your own practice' is more invitational and keeps it clear that these sessions are for the students themselves.

- Keep discussion of informal practice light and non-judgmental, perhaps simply enquiring whether anyone did anything helpful they might like to share. Avoid any sense of students having to 'prove' anything or hand in any written work.

- Suggest that students might use some good quality apps to guide their practice. Some mindfulness programmes include downloads of practices, and some schools develop their own. We list some apps that may be useful in Appendix 4.

- Most students will not want to engage with long practices on their own, although as the course progresses you might offer choice. Emphasise and be interested to hear about the use of short practices in everyday life, such as taking a few mindful breaths, or eating a few mindful mouthfuls.

The many small and routine ways young people use short 'grounding' practices can be motivating for others to hear about.

LEARNING FROM PROFESSIONAL PRACTICE
A secondary schools sets up a mindfulness peer mentor programme

We came up with a student mindfulness mentor scheme. Eight student mindfulness leaders applied and secured this role and have been since September 2019, once a fortnight at lunchtimes, training to teach staff and students in one-minute pocket mindfulness techniques. In future, they would like to guide others in their tutor group, guide their younger siblings, guide staff, re-visit our local primary school to lead practices and have also expressed an interest in possibly going into our local care home to guide any elderly 'people' who might want to learn some mindfulness practices from young people.

Sarah Gotting, Kings School, Devon

> **We have set up a quiet room for break and lunchtime use if students want to reflect, meditate, pray or just be still. This is a transformation.**

Assistant Head, Secondary School using the Jigsaw programme

TEACHING MINDFULNESS TO STUDENTS

Research shows that students often continue to practice themselves after the course has finished, usually in sporadic and informal ways, and particularly when facing personal challenges.[122] Some schools do not leave this to chance, but continue to offer mindfulness in other times and places, for example with:

- routine use of short 'moments of mindfulness' to bring everyone, students and staff, back to themselves. They can be used to punctuate the school day, especially at moments of transition.

- optional classes such as lunchtime clubs and drop-ins, sometimes in designated rooms.

- booster sessions for practice allocated within a specific lesson or tutor period each week to ensure continuation and development of practice.

- booster sessions during stressful periods such as examination preparation.

Using peer learning

Peer learning is an approach in which learners help one another learn. Those who advocate for peer learning see it as having value for encouraging active engagement, cooperation, autonomy and critical thinking in learners. It shifts the educational paradigm to be a process of active and participatory co-creation by engaged learners, rather than the passive acceptance of teacher-centred received wisdom.[123]

It is an inspirational and heart-warming moment when the young people have the confidence and skill to lead a practice and their fellow students quietly follow. Increasingly some schools are extending and formalising this process, using peer education to cultivate mindfulness in their school community. They are creating 'mindful champions' and 'mindfulness ambassadors' to deliver peer learning in down-to earth ways that are resonating with young people.

> **For young people who have experienced significant adversity, their stress system can be chronically activated. By building positive relationships first, we help the young people's stress system calm down and put in place this 'relational resource' before we then engage in mindfulness practice.**
>
> *Michael Bready, founder of Youth Mindfulness*

LEARNING FROM PROFESSIONAL PRACTICE

A fuss free approach when individual students don't want to participate in the meditation

I would advise a 20% drop out can be expected, sometimes more if the person who drops out is an 'influential' character. I have encouraged students to remain in the session by giving them permission to have a rest, even a snooze during the meditations. Sometimes they have even turned it around and ended up doing it anyway but pretending they aren't. I would also advise that for some it is simply too much to be in the room. I have asked those students to bring a book or load the Calm app on their phone.

Springboard special school, Letchworth Garden City

TEACHING MINDFULNESS TO STUDENTS

> **TOOLKIT**
> ### Creating a safe learning environment and safeguarding students
>
> Based on current recommendations for professional good practice in mindfulness, and the common sense of experienced classroom teachers, we offer the following advice, which incidentally mostly applies equally to teaching mindfulness to adults.
>
> - know the students and their circumstances well, including their personalities, sensitivities, home cultures, and past and current events in their lives.
>
> - anticipate that some may have problems that need special care to be taken, or even preclude doing mindfulness meditation altogether, such as recent bereavement, sexual abuse, or current serious mental health challenges.
>
> - agree on ground rules or class charter such as confidentiality, respect for opinions, and the 'right to pass'.
>
> - give alternatives to closing the eyes, such as using a soft gaze.
>
> - mention early on that some people find paying attention to sensations of breathing quite unsettling or uncomfortable, that this is quite normal, and suggest other potential 'anchors' such as the sensation of the feet on the floor.
>
> - help the class to practise finding a familiar 'safe place' to return to in longer meditations such as the breath or contact with the chair.
>
> - remind the class that mindfulness practice is an invitation not a command, and they can stop the practice completely and just sit quietly if they wish.
>
> - keep reflective enquiry invitational and avoid asking for any disclosures that may expose a student's 'soft underbelly' to possibly less than totally compassionate peers.
>
> - stay alert for obvious reactions – such as tearfulness, or withdrawal.
>
> - make further time to listen privately, ideally being routinely available after the class.
>
> - know the pastoral and support care system in the school well and refer on any major concerns promptly, following the school's child protection protocols. It is particularly important for outside facilitators to become aware of these routes.

> **66** My Year 6 class requested a Calm me time before they did their SATs papers. One of them went and got the chime and led the class through a mindfulness practice to calm and focus themselves. P.S. They did well in their SATs.

Primary teacher using the Jigsaw programme

TEACHING MINDFULNESS TO STUDENTS

Taking care of students and their vulnerabilities

There is an increasing concern within the mindfulness community of the need to take care and minimise the potential for harm, and research is rapidly developing on the issue. [124] There is some suggestion from small-scale qualitative research of possible occasional negative impacts of MBIs on vulnerable teens [125], but there is little hard evidence to date of any adverse effects from school-based mindfulness programmes for students. So far the balance of evidence suggests that well-delivered mindfulness programmes can in fact help with trauma.[126]

Nevertheless, mindfulness training programmes are increasingly and wisely becoming 'trauma informed', including for mainstream students. Current advice is that all teachers in schools, whatever their speciality, would do well to be trained in the relational principles of trauma-informed practice: these principles include building a sense of safety, connection, trustworthiness, collaboration, and empowerment, all of them the foundation of good teaching and effective relationships in classrooms. [127]

Mindfulness in schools needs to be seen as a low-key educational intervention rather than a therapeutic one. It is not intended to be seen as a substitute for therapy, medication or any of the wide range of appropriate actions that are needed to address acute mental health needs in young people, although it can support such actions.

Fitting mindfulness to the needs of students

Mindfulness needs to be delivered in a way that is appropriate for your students. In some schools the group may be fairly homogenous, but generally students are likely to come from many different social backgrounds and ethnicities and with differing abilities.

KEY ISSUE
Adapting for SEN students

When teaching SEN or ASD students or those with a diagnosis of mental health difficulties, it is essential that special considerations are made for their sensory, emotional and physical differences. Visuals that aren't too bright; practices that aren't too long; explanations that are simple; an environment that is considerate, familiar and comfortable; a teacher who is kind, compassionate and patient; and group numbers that are small. Quiet fidget toys are available for during practice, and time is allowed for 1:1 discussion at the end of the class.

Springboard special school, Letchworth Garden City

CHAPTER 9

Embedding and sustaining mindfulness within a whole school approach

Summary of Chapter 9

This chapter explores some of the ways in which schools are moving on from a model of mindfulness as a discrete Mindfulness-Based Intervention (MBI) to embedding and sustaining mindfulness across the processes, practices and ethos of the whole classroom and the whole school. The evidence and good practice suggest:

- a whole school approach, where all parts of the school and its community work smoothly together, has been shown to be the optimum setting for promoting wellbeing and developing social and emotional capacities in students and staff. Mindfulness has a core part to play in making this shift towards a more holistic approach a reality.

- mindfulness is being successfully embedded across schools in many areas including mental health and wellbeing, social and emotional learning, values such as kindness, compassion, connection with nature, neuroscience, the process of learning and the involvement of parents and the community. It provides an embodied and reflective grounding for areas of work that can otherwise tend to stay at the cognitive and verbal level.

- mindfulness can contribute to the development of connected and reflective school and classroom climates where staff and students experience and cultivate values such as kindness, compassion, respect, open-mindedness, tolerance, and mutual caring and responsibility.

> **99** **I love walking around the school hearing snippets of conversation between staff and pupils. Mindfulness and the different practices are creating a common language between staff and pupils, which is fantastic.**

Teacher in a school using the .b Mindfulness in Schools Project programme

EMBEDDING AND SUSTAINING MINDFULNESS WITHIN A WHOLE SCHOOL APPROACH

What is meant by a whole school approach?

There has recently been some empirical research around how to implement mindfulness within wider whole school approaches.[128] In this chapter we explore some ways in which mindfulness is starting to move on from being offered as discrete MBIs to becoming a more integral part of classroom and school processes.

The term 'whole school approach' is used in many different ways, including as a synonym for 'for everyone', for which a better term is 'universal'. In its origins, and in the research literature a whole school approach refers to efforts to create a joined up, multi-component and coherent environment and ethos, in which all parts of the school and its community work smoothly together.[129] Official guidance based on two decades of evidence[130], recommends a whole school approach for efforts to promote wellbeing, mental health and social and emotional learning in schools.[131]

Incorporating mindfulness as a key thread within whole school approaches is a particularly appropriate model, given its generic and foundational nature. This does not mean that mindfulness necessarily becomes the 'lead term' for the whole school approach: terms like 'wellbeing' may be more all-encompassing. Nor does it imply that everyone in the school is expected to learn and to formally practise mindfulness. It means that:

- mindfulness practice is accepted, recognised and practised as a dynamic cog in the engine of school life, one element among many others in the wider ecology of the classroom and school.

- the valuable human skills, capacities, attitudes and values which mindfulness helps cultivate are enhanced and grounded by its presence, as an integral and valuable part of many other complementary actions that also foster these qualities across the school community.

In mental health and wellbeing

Mindfulness can help position mental health and wellbeing of staff and students at the heart of school life.

The evidence for the impact of mindfulness on positive wellbeing and on mental health, for students and staff, and case study examples of it working in practice are reviewed in Chapter 2. This is the area on which most of the programmes to be found in the UK focus most strongly.

Many schools now use a 'toolkit' approach of initiatives such as mental health 'first aid'. This is a good start in a crisis but does not go as deep as it might. Mindfulness can help school members to build the inner skills and capacities that support mental health on a more long-term basis. More widely it can encourage and support a holistic and systems-based approach to mental health and wellbeing across the school. This approach applies equally to teachers teachers as well as students. It emphasises the meaningfulness of distressed behaviour, including that which schools experience as 'difficult', the importance of relationships, the significance of the school process itself for good or ill, awareness of the reality of trauma, and the complexity of underlying social, structural and contextual causes.

In social and emotional learning

It can help mindfulness to have more leverage, relate more clearly to school's work on promoting wellbeing, and provide a context and a sense of relevance if it is supported by and embedded in other elements of the curriculum.

The area of the curriculum into which mindfulness is most often linked, and sometimes embedded, is what is known internationally and in the research as 'social and emotional learning' (SEL).

> **What we are really trying to do is to make a school become a second family where the teacher, the students, and the whole school—the parents as well—see it as a joint effort—a joint effort to create a place where it's not all about the future, about your career, job, position, or your money, but a place where you actually enjoy living and enjoy learning, and enjoy exploring, right now.**

Br Phap Dung from Happy Teachers Change the World, by Thich Nhat Hanh and Katherine Weare

According to CASEL, the network responsible for developing this work in the US, SEL refers to *'the process through which all young people and adults acquire and apply the knowledge, skills, and attitudes to develop healthy identities, manage emotions and achieve personal and collective goals, feel and show empathy for others, establish and maintain supportive relationships, and make responsible and caring decisions'.*[132]

The constantly shifting terminology around this area across the four countries that make up the UK currently includes Health and Wellbeing (Wales, Northern Ireland, and Scotland) Personal and Social Education (Wales and England) 'Wellbeing and Relationship Based Education' (Scotland) Personal Development, Relationships and Sex education, and Spiritual, Moral, Social and Cultural development (England). Other looser generic terms include character, values, life skills, resilience, happiness, and wellbeing.

As there is no one agreed UK-wide term, we will use the term SEL here, a term routinely used in schools in Northern Ireland.

Whatever its current name, this whole area has gone in and out of favour in comparison with the traditional curriculum, as different governments come and go. It has traditionally often been something of a 'Cinderella' area in UK 3-18 education, particularly in England. There are signs it is now achieving greater prominence: for example in England the new Ofsted framework for Personal Development requires schools to pay attention to and report on it[133] and there is a new 'Curriculum for Wellbeing' in Wales.[134] All of these are opportunities for mindfulness to have a core role.

How does mindfulness relate to SEL?

Teaching mindfulness as part of SEL can be a particularly apt fit, given the congruence of ultimate aims. The evidence (outlined in Chapter 2) suggests that mindfulness practice can cultivate social and emotional skills and qualities including self-awareness, self-regulation, resilience, relationship skills, empathy, compassion, and a sense of social responsibility.

Mindfulness is often described as the 'key' or 'missing piece' of SEL. The relationship between mindfulness and SEL has been most thoroughly explored in the US where the two fields are well developed, often by the same innovation teams and within the same programmes.[135] As the table of programmes in Appendix 1 shows, some UK-based programmes, such as Jigsaw, the mindful approach to PSHE (ages 3-16) and some programmes in the UK that originated in the US, such as MindUp, integrate mindfulness into work on SEL from the outset.

> **"At present, mindfulness plays a key role in all our PSE lessons across the 3-16 community. Teachers will often participate in the mindfulness practice alongside the learners showing good role modelling and to help with their own personal wellbeing. There are a team of PSE teachers who deliver Jigsaw and mindfulness to ensure there is consistency.**
>
> *Abertillery Learning Community, Blaenau Gwent*

To suggest what mindfulness brings to SEL:

- Through its present moment, embodied, skills-based approach, mindfulness can help ensure that the aims of SEL are realised in practice and action, not just expressed as theories, words and future intentions.

- SEL can be somewhat solution focused. In contrast, mindfulness does not immediately focus on outcomes such as finding an answer to a dilemma or feeling better: it offers an alternative response to difficulties that cannot immediately be 'solved'.

- Mindfulness adds the ability to be fully present and non-reactive, in body as well as mind, with whatever is happening, including with uncertainty and unpleasant emotions. This can help build patience, resilience and insight - often more realistic and valuable responses to life's dilemmas than knee-jerk reactions.

The danger of combining mindfulness and SEL in one programme is a dilution of the core nature and authenticity of mindfulness. If mindfulness is to make this unique contribution it is important that it is taught in its fullest sense, as including but being more than just 'relaxing', 'calming' or even 'paying attention', all of which can easily become a form of simplistic 'fix it'. The core integrity of mindfulness, as forming a new relationship to experience, approaching what is happening in the present moment, including the difficult, with open-minded kindness and curiosity as the basis for wiser action needs to be firmly in place.

> **Mindfulness had been drip fed gently throughout the whole school these last few years, and we have embedded the values of mindfulness with all pupils and staff.**
>
> Culcross Primary, School Fife

Within work on key values: compassion, gratitude and connection

Education is not morally neutral. Schools routinely take time to clarify and promote their core values and to teach them to students. UK schools are increasingly encouraged explicitly to cultivate certain values in their students to help create more civil and democratic societies. These values include tolerance, the defence of human rights, the protection of vulnerable groups, the conservation of the environment, and efforts to tackle the climate crisis.

Mindfulness has a key role to play in this process, particularly through its emphasis on developing the skills and attitudes that underlie human values such as kindness, compassion, gratitude and connection. Mindfulness courses are starting to add an explicit component of compassion practice. This is having an enhanced impact on many aspects of wellbeing and sociability in teachers and students, including self-care, resilience, optimism, positivity, the ability to take account of the impact of one's own behaviour on others, and not take the behaviour of others so personally.

Mindfulness and compassion are starting to be taught together, and mindfulness is starting to move into newer areas including the cultivation of gratitude and forgiveness. Some mindfulness programmes, such as the MiSP cluster of programmes, now include these issues in their core curriculum. There are some well-established programmes such as Mind with Heart Wake Up Schools which focus on compassion explicitly, and others, such as the Compassionate Mind Foundation at the University of Derby are developing rapidly. (See the table of programmes in Appendix 1).

Mindfulness and nature

Mindfulness links easily with efforts to encourage a sense of interconnectedness with nature, ecology and the wider environment. It is starting to appear in movements such as Forest Schools, Nature Friendly Schools, Outdoor Education, Animal Assisted Therapy and similar movements, where its value in helping children and young people connect more directly with the natural world through helping them pay close attention to their experience is becoming apparent.

> **We've created an inset training day for teachers engaged in Forest Schools and Outdoor Learning. Being mindful in nature helps teachers and pupils connect more with their senses and nurture their interest in their personal experiences with nature. The 'Wow Practice' celebrates children's natural curiosity while the 'Selfie Practice' prompts them to map their internal landscape while in the outdoors. We find mindfulness practice in this context boosts their sense of connection and appreciation of the environment. Feedback is very positive.**
>
> Tim Anfield, Mindful Families

> **One boy told me, after yet another crisis, 'My amygdala was too quick for me!'. At least now he has some understanding of what's happening to him when the panic begins.**

Llwyncrwn Primary School, Pontypridd

With neuroscience education

Chapter 3 outlines some of the underlying neuroscience, including what we know about the changes in brain and body structure and function that mindfulness can bring. We explore in that chapter some of the reasons why this so-called 'brain-based learning' is now growing in educational thinking and in schools.

Programmes of mindfulness in schools, and social and emotional learning more generally, often now integrate simple neuroscience into their content and include straightforward psychology and neuroscience. This can help students and teachers:

- understand the physiology and psychology of their own minds, including how the brain and nervous system work, and the workings of the structures involved in underlying processes like self-regulation and the stress response.

- be aware of and able to label the inner processes going on in the brain and the body that underlie their mental and physical states and behaviour, such as metacognition and compassion.

> **My proudest moment was when the Head of Year 11 asked me if it was ok to put a large '.b' on the inside cover of their year book because it was the thing that had most resonated with them that year (.b is a short practice from the MiSP curriculum).**

Amanda Bailey, Star Academies

Within the process of learning

Chapter 2 explores the evidence for the impact of mindfulness on learning, and Chapter 3 explores the mechanisms through which this works and impacts on skills underlying effective learning, such as attention, self-regulation, and metacognition.

These generic skills are increasingly of interest to mainstream educators and explicitly cultivated in schools. The Education Endowment Fund has recently produced a review and guidance on why and how metacognition and self-regulation need to be at the heart of the teaching and learning process.[136] Mindfulness can help realise the aims of this area of work in the folllowing ways:

- mindfulness explicitly expands the model of teaching and learning from one that is about imparting a given body of knowledge from 'out there' to one which puts the learner at the centre. It empowers learners, by enabling them to appreciate first-hand what is happening in the moment, clearly and directly, in their thoughts, feelings and bodily reactions as they engage more critically and reflectively in the act of learning.

- mindfulness can enable work on the process of learning which is often taught as a predominantly verbal and cognitive approach, to be more grounded in the totality of the mind, heart and body of the learner. It can include and integrate embodied sensory and emotional experience alongside thinking processes.

Embedding mindfulness practice directly within teaching and learning in the mainstream curriculum is an approach that is often found under the heading 'contemplative education' or 'contemplative pedagogy'. This approach has been described as 'mindfulness _as_ education', rather than mindfulness _in_ education.[137] It is more fully developed in higher education than school but has great potential in moving mindfulness into the heart of the educational process in both sectors.

EMBEDDING AND SUSTAINING MINDFULNESS WITHIN A WHOLE SCHOOL APPROACH

> **LEARNING FROM PROFESSIONAL PRACTICE**
> **A primary school establishes 'mindful practice as the central tenet of teaching and learning'**
>
> Mindful practices such as glitter bottles, reflect and respond and yoga lessons are now a standard practice of the school, allowing children to calm, become more motivated and regulate emotions and actions. The school has now developed even further, establishing mindful practices as a central tenet of its teaching and learning practices. The new Learning 4 Life curriculum includes the importance of mindful practices including self-awareness, self-reflection and self-regulation and has a focus on character skills alongside pupils developing academic skills and knowledge.
>
> Mindfulness is now an intrinsic part of the school's ethos. Reflection is a whole school value and reflects the commitment to the school in nurturing children's talents, engagement and interests in a holistic manner. Mindfulness and wellbeing strategies underpin the curriculum and are seen as skills children need to underpin their academic skills. This now pervades across subject areas with reflection being valued as part of feedback in lessons and allowing children time to pause and think in lessons, to deepen their learning and knowledge.
>
> *Eyres Monstall Primary School, Leicester*

Involving parents and the wider community

Schools often report that they find it invaluable to include governors, parents and other members of the surrounding community in the school's mindfulness journey, to keep them informed and to invite them in at key points.

Mindfulness is likely to be attractive and intriguing to parents, most of whom will have at least heard of it and some of whom may practice it themselves. Indeed, in some schools it is pressure from parents who practise that has set the ball rolling. Schools may initially face concerns from some parents who need reassuring about myths and misconceptions.

Mindfulness often makes its way home via the children. Parents may see any materials brought home in schoolbags, while students often report that they talk to their families about mindfulness, and use the skills at home, particularly when things get difficult.

Mindfulness for parents and parenting is a growing field in its own right. Some schools teach mindfulness to parents and some mindfulness programmes include 'family mindfulness' in their offering, containing elements that teach parents mindfulness for their own wellbeing.

> **"** In the latter phases, support for parents and the local community has become more important, with mindful sessions for parents and carers being offered and the introduction of Jigsaw Families, to support loving relationships within the home. The school also offer tea and talk and Brew Monday, to encourage openness and connectedness within its wider school community.
>
> *Eyres Monsell Primary School, Leicester*

Embedding and sustaining in classroom and school climate, culture and ethos

In some classrooms and some schools, mindfulness is gradually becoming embedded within aspects of the whole school as a system, including its language, policies, procedures, curriculum, staff development, student involvement and liaison with parents.

Mindfulness also impacts on the powerful elements of school values, ecology, climate, and ethos. This is particularly through its impacts on teacher effectiveness in classrooms, which we explored in Chapter 3.

Normalising mindfulness practice, and the open-minded and kindly attitudes it cultivates can help it to gradually become an integral part of 'how we do things here'.

A congruent working environment

A whole school approach, which embeds mindfulness in school processes and ethos, invariably starts and ends with the school staff. The working environment needs to support and facilitate staff engaging in mindfulness practice, and more fundamentally 'walk the talk' by promoting their mental health and wellbeing through the ethos of kindness and care that is fundamental to the attitudes mindfulness cultivates.[138]

The senior leadership team can support this by ensuring that they model taking care of their own wellbeing as leaders, and allowing time and space for staff self-care, paying attention to features such as sensible and ethical workload practices, humane performance management procedures, open, honest communication, and democratic and reflective leadership.

LEARNING FROM PROFESSIONAL PRACTICE
Mindfulness becomes embedded as 'a way of life' for an organisation working with hard to reach youth

Mindfulness is a way of life at Raise. It is not something just for the children. It is integrated into the way we operate, and embedded as a whole school approach, supporting our children, young people and staff. Doing the work we do can be tough for staff and mindfulness provides the tools to self-regulate, to be able to do their best for the children. It gives us all space to reflect. We've trained everyone, from teachers, directors, TAs, social workers to our cleaners, finance and administration teams. Our work can be challenging and mindfulness enables us to extend non-judgement and kindness to all the people we deal with on behalf of the children. This helps us to achieve better outcomes whilst looking after ourselves. I also feel that our mindful approach has an impact on the other agencies we deal with, and the wider community recognises the values we have.

Jason Steele CEO, Raise The Youth (Raise works to improve the prospects of hard to reach youngsters from 11-25)

LEARNING FROM PROFESSIONAL PRACTICE
Embedding mindfulness across the whole school

The Kids Programme was stand-alone, however, elements from the course were then embedded within the school. The class teacher now leads regular meditations with the class. Language around mindfulness has been embedded. Children talk about 'noticing and allowing', they are able to pay attention to their emotions and name them. They are encouraged to reflect so they can notice patterns of behaviour and become more aware. The children go on regular mindful walks. Body scans are used after sport to allow the children time to calm before going back to class. Gratitude and kindness are also key areas within the course and children are much more aware of their effect on others. So, it's really embedded and there's a common vocabulary between pupils and staff because so many members of staff have done it. It's something that the pupils know they do and it's something that they can hear their older peers talking about and it's something that has a real currency in the school. I think it really is sustainable in its current form.

Culcross Primary School, Fife

> **KEY ISSUE**
> ## Working within the framework and languages of existing national educational policies on wellbeing
>
> In order for mindfulness to be embedded across a whole school, it helps if it's seen as a priority for the senior leadership team and school's governing body. For that to be the case, mindfulness needs to work within the framework and languages of current education policies across the UK. There has been a shift in recent years in UK education policy towards schools promoting the mental health and wellbeing of students and staff, particularly, at the time of writing, around the fallout for young people and schools from the COVID-19 crisis.
>
> ### Wales
>
> The *New Curriculum for Wales*, to be fully implemented in primary and Y7 from 2022, provides a framework within which schools or groups of schools will develop their curriculum to deliver 'What Matters' in six areas of learning and experience, including Health and Wellbeing. Mindfulness has the potential to make a significant contribution to these developments, and practitioners across the country have been developing a Mindfulness Toolkit as guidance on implementing effective mindfulness strategies. This is underpinned by the far-reaching *Wellbeing of Future Generations Act* creating a wider context for developing a kinder, more compassionate and sustainable society. *Mindfulness Wales* has been set up to explore and develop best practice in mindfulness in education, health, community and more.
>
> ### Scotland
>
> The *Curriculum for Excellence* in Scotland has been in existence since 2010, and one of its eight strands is focused on health and wellbeing. The curriculum specifically states that health and wellbeing is as important as numeracy and literacy, and these three areas are the responsibility of all staff. There is a particular priority given by the government to identifying and responding to *adverse childhood experience* to which mindfulness programmes are responding.
>
> ### England
>
> The 2017 Green Paper *Transforming Children and Young People's Mental Health* made student wellbeing a major priority for the government, with every school and college being supported to train a *senior mental health* lead by 2025. The new Ofsted framework introduced in 2019 has a greater focus on what schools are doing to support staff wellbeing as well as inspecting for what schools are doing to increase learners' *'resilience, confidence and independence – and to help them know how to keep physically and mentally healthy'*. Additionally, from September 2020, relationships education (primary) and relationships and sex education (secondary) will be mandatory in all state schools, and the health education aspect includes teaching children about mental health and wellbeing (including strategies for developing self-regulation) as part of a whole school approach. These are ripe opportunities for mindfulness to play a part in improving the mental health and wellbeing of teaching staff and students.
>
> ### Northern Ireland
>
> In 2012, the *Protecting Children* guidance was updated, and a focus was placed on identifying children with mental health difficulties, as well as a need for schools and teachers to promote positive mental health. The 'Big Picture' of the secondary curriculum also indicates the importance of students developing 'self-management', 'concern for others', 'curiosity' and 'openness to new ideas'.

CHAPTER 10

Evaluating mindfulness in a school

Summary of Chapter 10

This chapter aims to demystify the research process and encourage schools to consider evaluating their efforts at mindfulness. It suggests:

- Evaluation needs to be based on a clear idea of how the evaluation data will be used in practice, how it relates to the school's priorities, how the process will involve and empower the community, and what capacity the school has to undertake it.

- It is important to evaluate acceptability (the extent to which an input is popular and meets immediate needs) if mindfulness is to develop and be sustained.

- Process evaluation/action research is a model that fits well with existing school routines for collecting and using data for school improvement.

- Quantitative approaches (e.g. before and after designs and controlled trials) and qualitative approaches (e.g. interviews and focus groups) both working together, can provide value for schools in improving practice and in the data they gather to help build confidence in mindfulness, through compelling both numbers and through stories.

- There is plenty of online support, including packages to design, administer and analyse both quantitative and qualitative approaches.

This chapter is supported by Appendix 3, an annotated list of the measures and tools regularly used.

Before starting – questions a school might use for initial reflection

- Have we clearly identified our needs and priorities? Are the changes we hope mindfulness can help make realistic and in line with the evidence?

- How are we going to use the data? To improve our mindfulness rollout and its outcomes, for accountability, to advertise the impacts of mindfulness in our school to relevant stakeholders?

- Can we engage our whole school community in carrying out our research effort, so the process can take people with us and not feel like an imposition?

- Can we collect data before we start any changes? (If built in at the outset, data gathering is easier and results more definitive.)

- What type of design, methods, analysis and write-up do we realistically have the skills and capacity to use? (Less is probably more.)

Evaluating acceptability

Assessing so called 'acceptability' is essential, as unless your colleagues and students appreciate the intervention, believe it meets their needs, and eventually report that it is making a perceptible and valued change, there is not much hope of positive measurable outcomes or of the intervention being sustained.[139]

Collecting systematic feedback on acceptability can help you discover and track the impact of inputs on people's thoughts, feelings, intentions, actions, and concerns and provide systematically collected data to guide improvements. Following up on negative views can help make the intervention better, ensure it works for as many people as possible, and ensure it is not inadvertently doing harm.

Explore further

Assessing acceptability does not have to be an overcomplicated process, as simple examples and a template from the Mindfulness in Schools project show: https://mindfulnessinschools.org/participant-feedback/

LEARNING FROM PROFESSIONAL PRACTICE

A primary teacher constructs a simple questionnaire - the responses are 'eye opening'

In house research needs to be useful and not over complicated. A primary teacher describes the process of constructing a simple questionnaire about how children are using mindfulness, and the eye-opening value of the responses.

'I took these aims (of the Mindfulness in Schools Project) and created a brief online questionnaire, asking the children from my previous classes to respond. I also used some questions similar to those used in the MiSP impact survey.

The response was heartening: 95% said that they had enjoyed doing the Paws b course when they were in my class. They remembered most of the practices, and two-thirds of them still use them at least sometimes. Five children revealed that they practise daily. I had no idea.

The survey further revealed that the children used the practices to help them in many different ways.....most revealing of all, perhaps, was the fact that only half the children surveyed knew about the Mindfulness Club - and 27 of them said they would like to come! So, there was a lesson to be learned for me about getting the news 'out there' about the opportunities for mindfulness in school.'

Matthew Jones, Acting Assistant Head at Llwyncryn Primary School Pontypridd, South Wales

Evaluation as a process – action research

It is helpful to see evaluation and implementation as a process, a cycle or spiral, rather than just as a one-off measurement of an end point or outcome. A useful model is action research, a spiral of steps, each of which is composed of a 'circle of planning, action and fact-finding about the result of the action.'[140] It seeks transformative change through the simultaneous process of taking action and doing research, processes which are linked together by critical reflection. It has a close resemblance to the school improvement process with which schools will be familiar.[141]

This model of evaluation as a process fits in well in a school which is dedicated to the concept of actively listening to, and engaging with, its whole community, to a culture of continuous improvement, and with the routine use of formative as well as summative assessment of their students.[142] It can encourage your school to work in a collaborative way, and build engagement, rather than risk your evaluation feeling like something remote which is 'done to' people.

These are the typical stages of the action research cycle

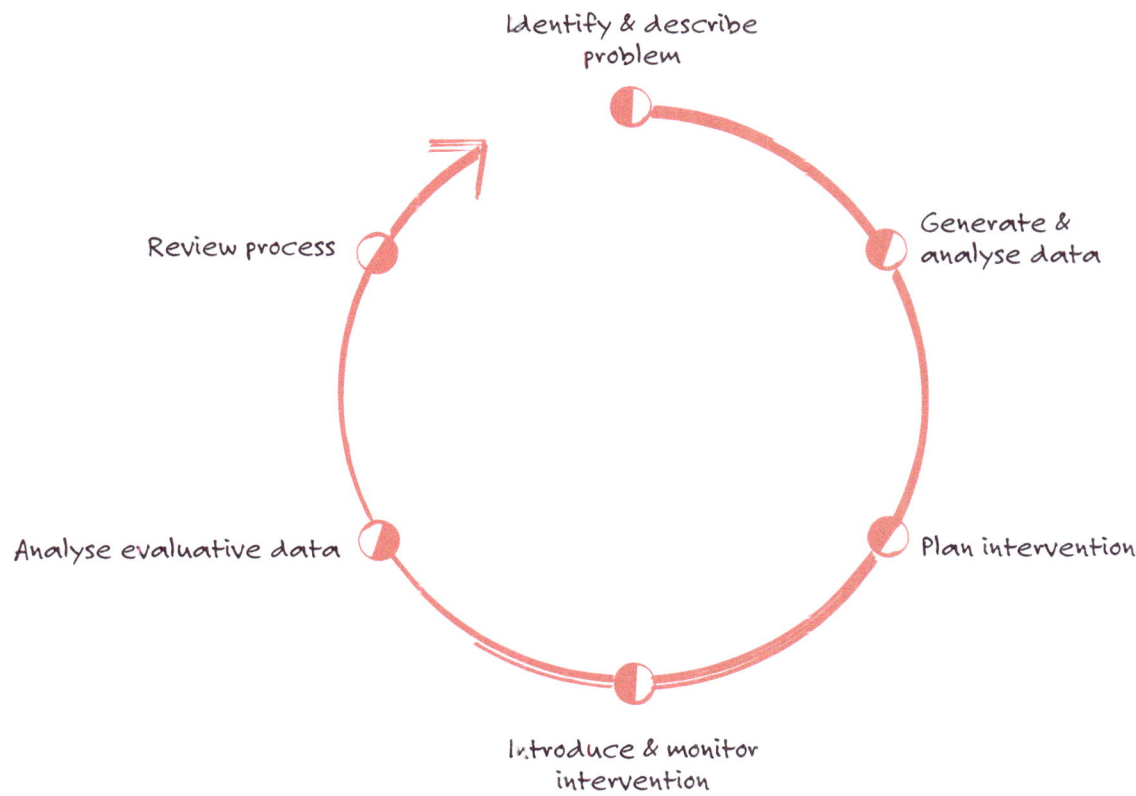

It is tempting to only look at outcomes, but action research can answer a range of interesting questions around implementation:

- What was the effect of the intervention on attitudes, beliefs, behaviour of participants? Did this change at different time points?

- Who did it work well for, who not so well? Why might that be?

- What affected the uptake and implementation of the intervention?

- Was the intervention delivered as planned? If there were adaptations, what was their rationale and their impact?

- How can we improve this intervention in light of these findings?

EVALUATING MINDFULNESS IN A SCHOOL

The value of both quantitative and qualitative data

- Quantitative approaches answer questions such as what, who and how many? They are usually fairly quick to use, produce data that are easy to compare and analyse and transformable into numbers, charts, graphs, and tables. Write-ups of quantitative data tend to go down well with funders and the inspectorate, as they are seen as objective and reliable.

- Qualitative research seeks to understand people's lived experience from the inside, and answers questions such as 'how?' and 'why?'. Qualitative approaches can get behind the numerical data and tell you how the outcomes were arrived at, or how to improve things. They are useful in influencing others, because people tend to respond better to words and stories than they do to graphs and numbers: qualitative research can provide first-hand experiences and stories that can be moving, persuasive, and engaging.

> **If pupils are talking about mindfulness positively and/or suggesting its use then this piques staff interest further.**
>
> *Amanda Bailey, Star Academies*

- Evaluation is most useful and effective when it makes use of both quantitative and qualitative methods.

Quantitative methods and designs

Before and after

- Before and after/pre-post test is an experimental type study design where the measurements are taken before and after an intervention.

- It can be carried out with no controls or with a control group. A control group is a matching group who do not receive the intervention. Selecting who goes in which group can in turn be unrandomised or randomised.

- Before and after studies without controls can be useful, particularly as a pilot or feasibility study to test out the intervention, to see if the process works, and if any interim outcomes are in the right direction. It is not as robust as a design that uses a control as there is no way to know what other events and trends happening in the surrounding environment may be impacting on results, e.g. a parallel intervention, a stressful Ofsted inspection, or simply students getting older.

Control trials/randomised control trials (RCTs)

- A control trial (CT) divides people interested in undertaking the Mindfulness-Based Intervention (MBI) into two groups: an 'experimental' group (who will undertake the MBI) and a 'control' group. The control group will not do the MBI in the trial, although ideally to keep up motivation they do so later, a so called 'wait list' design.

- In a classic RCT, individual participants are allocated to the different groups by blind random selection to reduce bias. This may not often be be possible in school settings where target respondents foten come as whole classes, but maybe possible where people come as individuals, such as school staff, SEN students or those receiving counselling.

- In school settings it is more usual for randomisation to be by school class i.e. classes are chosen blindly and at random to receive the intervention or not. It is important to try to ensure that classes are as similar as possible, e.g., in the same school, the same age and ability range. The classes that missed out may receive the intervention later.

- Assessments should ideally be conducted at three time points: before, immediately after, and follow up (three months is classic) and for both groups.

Appendix 3 is a list of measures most frequently used in school contexts to assess the impacts of MBIs, focusing particularly on those used in the UK.

Explore further

A useful online tool to help schools carry out a before and after evaluation can be found at the Early Intervention website https://educationendowmentfoundation.org.uk/tools/diy-guide/getting-started/

A useful introduction to planning and conducting an RCT is available at http://betterevaluation.org/plan/approach/rct

Qualitative methods and designs

There are many approaches to qualitative research and they all tend to be flexible and focus on retaining rich meaning when interpreting data. They usually involve collecting data in the form of language, asking participants about their experience using semi-structured or open-ended methods. Methods of data collection include:

- one-to-one interview with a researcher.

- a focus group.

- participant observation: observing what happens in natural settings such as a playground, staffroom or classroom.

- written: free response boxes in a questionnaire, journals, diaries etc.

Write-ups of qualitative research are sometimes known as case studies. These are intensive studies of an individual, or more commonly a group of people, which aim to outline their views and understandings in ways that are potentially generalisable to other similar people or places.

The language-based raw data, such as from interviews or focus groups, are typically audio-recorded and then transcribed. The resulting data are then subject to various forms of analysis.

- The method most often used in a school evaluation is content analysis or thematic analysis, which is the process of looking for common content and themes across the transcripts. (We endnote other more complex methods of analysis of qualitative data[143].)

- The process does not have to be overcomplicated to give useful results, but it does need to be transparent and systematic, and it is sensible to have a team involved to check for consistency and bias.

The write-up of thematic or content analysis:

- sets out the dominant themes, patterns and frequencies and may tentatively suggest some possible cause and effect linkages.

- outlines the varieties of opinion within a group, and indicates how understandings, stories, ideas and themes may hang together.

- sometimes makes a broad numeric calculation of the weight of opinion and feeling.

- usually includes a good deal of verbatim quotation.

If a school wants to carry out a larger scale qualitative study, there is plenty of advice available on the web, and some university-based online courses to teach the necessary skills. The process of analysing larger quantities of qualitative data has been made easier by the development of computer packages such as NVivo and ATLAS-ti[144].

Who might carry out a more complex evaluation?

- **In house:** there may be one or more people on the staff, or in the school's wider community, such as parents, governors, or an educational psychologist, who have the time, motivation, training and competence in educational research, and in collecting, managing and analysing the data: words, numbers and statistics.

- A **local university** may have i) the ability to offer consultancy and/or ii) research students who might like the opportunity to use the school as a context for their research. This will also help you to remain more objective and unbiased.

EVALUATING MINDFULNESS IN A SCHOOL

> **EXPLORE FURTHER**
> **Online resources**
>
> Simple quantitative and qualitative studies can be carried out fairly easily with the help of online resources.
>
> - 'Bounce together' is a digital platform for measuring and continually monitoring the wellbeing, behaviours, health, perceptions and attitudes of a school's students and staff https://www.bouncetogether.co.uk/. It may be appropriate to use where a school wants to evaluate mindfulness as part of wider work on wellbeing.
>
> - 'DIY Evaluation Guide' is an online tool to help schools carry out a before and after evaluation on any topic, including mindfulness, developed by the well respected Early Endowment Foundation https://educationendowmentfoundation.org.uk/tools/diy-guide/getting-started/.
>
> - SurveyMonkey https://www.surveymonkey.com/ can help construct a simple questionnaire, turn findings into a range of different graphics and graphs, and be exportable into databases such as Excel.
>
> - A free interactive short course 'Measuring mental wellbeing to improve the lives of children and young people' aims to demystify and simplify the whole process of using outcomes and feedback measures to monitor mental wellbeing, and can be applied equally to measuring mindfulness. https://www.corc.uk.net/elearning/.

LEARNING FROM PROFESSIONAL PRACTICE
A primary school uses an online tool to assess wellbeing, including mindfulness

In the school I work in, as a teacher and wellbeing lead governor, we take the happiness and wellbeing of our school community seriously. As well as embedding wellbeing into our curriculum (we teach the Paws b course from Year 4 upwards and use the Jigsaw resources in our PSHE lessons), we also started to measure the wellbeing of pupils and staff. We used the questions in the **Good Childhood Index for pupils** (short version) and the **What Works Centre for Wellbeing Employee Snapshot Survey** as the basis for anonymous self-completion surveys. We informed pupils that if answering the survey brought up any difficult feelings, there was a member of staff available to speak with them.

The school used an online tool called **Bounce Together** to administer the surveys, provide results and to help us analyse the data (which made the process less onerous and time-consuming than it otherwise might have been). Administering and analysing the results through an online tool proved to be easy. Being able to share the findings and plans for improvement has proved invaluable, for example at governors' meetings.

We have found out some new and important information, for example that physical health among staff had one of the lowest scores. We consulted further with staff to find out how the school could support them and have provided them with subsidised gym memberships, and the school sports coach is putting on staff fitness sessions after school for those who wish to attend.

Carrying out the research itself has been motivating. It has also proved popular with staff and pupils with some colleagues saying they appreciated taking the time to reflect on their lives and levels of wellbeing, and many children saying things like, 'That was fun! When will we do the survey again?'. It has shown us that we shouldn't underestimate the importance of asking children and teaching staff how they are feeling, really listening to their responses and then acting on their feedback.

Our plan is to repeat the baseline survey at the beginning and end of each academic year, to see if any trends emerge, to identify what we can do as a school to support our staff, children and their families, and to gauge the impact of our wellbeing-related work.

Adrian Bethune, Broughton Junior School, Aylesbury

> ### 📖 EXPLORE FURTHER
> ### Some further sources of support for evaluation
>
> **On evaluating mindfulness**
>
> 'Making sure it works' which is section 5 of the 'Fieldbook for Mindfulness Innovators' by The Mindfulness Initiative gives practical advice on the application and evaluation of mindfulness.
> https://www.themindfulnessinitiative.org/fieldbook-for-mindfulness-innovators
>
> **On evaluating wellbeing**
>
> A useful basic set of guidelines on measuring and monitoring, including links to 30 scales focusing on mental health and wellbeing, has been produced by Public Health England with the Anna Freud Centre. 'Measuring and monitoring children and young people's mental wellbeing: A toolkit for schools and colleges'.
> https://www.annafreud.org/media/4612/mwb-toolki-final-draft-4.pdf
>
> **On the research process**
>
> Education Research That Matters: Ways of Researching is a free online course on educational research methods developed by the University of Birmingham https://www.futurelearn.com/courses/ways-of-researching
>
> The Educational Endowment Fund team of Regional Leads provides local support to develop Partnerships with their 37-strong network of Research Schools. These schools share their knowledge and expertise on effective teaching and provide evidence-informed support and training to bring research closer to schools in their area. Support for schools | Education Endowment Foundation | EEF https://educationendowmentfoundation.org.uk/

POST-SCRIPT

Some thoughts on where next for mindfulness in schools

This final section outlines some of the ways in which mindfulness in schools might most usefully evolve to be of clear value in the effort to help education to face the challenges of our rapidly changing world.

The immediate priorities: embedding in school contexts

For mindfulness in schools to play a foundational role in educational and social transformation, it has first actually to be there as a strong presence in educational contexts. To help become a reality its value and relevance need to be clearer to schools. As approaches to mindfulness move on from their origins in health settings into a variety of new contexts (which currently include schools and other educational settings, the workplace, the family, and the criminal justice system) mindfulness needs to develop to be more closely aligned to the understandings, needs, processes, priorities, style and language of these new environments.

At present modern mindfulness remains strongly shaped by the medical model, 'delivered' as discrete, brief, one off 'interventions' and evaluated in terms of measurable outcomes, often by randomised control trial methodologies. The model of mindfulness as an intervention has a clear value, including in education, as the review of the evidence base outlined in Section 2 shows. It gives mindfulness a strong and measurable credibility on which future developments can be built. However to move more to the centre of the educational process, and gain traction and power, mindfulness needs to become more strongly shaped by the process, culture, values and ethos of education, classrooms and schools.

Some specific areas of educational embedding that are currently emerging include the following. They have all been discussed in Section 3 of this guidance and with some promising real life examples of good practice in schools:

- Teaching and learning will inevitably remain the main 'business' of schools: mindfulness needs to build more foundations in this area if it is to be seen as core and not peripheral. It would be useful to develop further the concept of mindfulness as education rather than being restricted to mindfulness in education. Mindfulness as education puts mindfulness and its reflective, embodied practice at the heart of the teaching and learning process. It links with areas of increasing interest to education, including metacognition, cognitive regulation and critical thinking[145].

- Mindfulness can develop a stronger relationship with complementary areas already on the rise in education and which focus on the development of the whole person, including their inner life. They include social and emotional learning, emotional regulation, self-regulation, resilience, character and values, and movement-based practice such as yoga.

- Mindfulness can also forge better links with initiatives in schools that foster a sense of connection between the person and their social and natural environment. This can both nourish us all in the here and now, and enable us to be empowered to contribute to efforts to tackle the environmental crisis, biodiversity and climate chaos. Some current growth areas include compassion, ecology, and nature-based learning.

- Mindfulness in education can usefully make more links with mindfulness in related contexts, particularly with organisational and workplace mindfulness, through links with teacher wellbeing and mindful leadership, and with mindful parenting.

- To reflect the growing concern with diversity, equality and social justice, mindfulness interventions and inputs in schools need now to move on from 'one size fits all' to becoming more culturally and developmentally responsive to differences - in gender, race, ethnicity, culture, age, abilities and disabilities.

- As mindfulness develops in school contexts, a wide range of models of teacher preparation have emerged that have diverged from the lengthy and criterion based preparation offered to those who train to teach mindfulness to adults in health contexts. Some models used in the school context are intensive, some lighter, and sometimes there is no preparation, just the provision of resources for teachers to use with students. There is a need to determine what type, length and intensity of preparation, and further ongoing support, produce an adequately competent teacher of mindfulness in schools who is effective, able to minimise the risk of any harm being done, and for what level of instruction. This is most appropriately determined by empirical research on the demonstrated outcomes of different approaches, not driven by economic considerations only.

- Mindfulness could usefully develop a greater focus on suitable ways to teach mindfulness to the vulnerable: this can help to ensure that mindfulness taught by schoolteachers in universal contexts to whole classes, rather than by therapists to those who choose freely to attend, takes care to minimise harm. We need to better understand how appropriate teacher education can make this safeguarding a reality, and then apply this knowledge in classrooms.

Mindfulness has a core role in helping education respond to 21st century challenges

We have argued that mindfulness is foundational to education: it follows that the future of mindfulness in schools is tied into the role and future of education as whole.

Education is being seen at all levels, including by global organizations such as UNESCO [146], as the single most powerful transformative force to help build a humane, just and sustainable world in the face of hitherto unimaginable global and existential challenges. The interrelated challenges facing us all include social injustice, a rise in authoritarianism and extremism, the threat of runaway technology, public health emergencies and, most fundamentally of all, the threat to existence caused by human transgression of planetary limits. At the same time, we are experiencing dangerous countercurrents that undermine humanity's ability to face these issues. These include a loss of belief in science, truth and public organisations, accompanied by social fragmentation and polarisation.

It has been argued that this predicament stems from the consequences of our own progress, such as the unbridled adoption of social media and other internet technologies, whilst not better developing ourselves in order to handle this extra complexity. To develop our own ability to meet these challenges it is becoming increasingly clear that we need more investment in the cultural and psychological resources that underpin a healthy social fabric, and a functional body politic, including through the medium of effective lifelong education.

There is no shortage of suggestions about what shifts are needed for education to cultivate the so called '21st century skills', and the values and attitudes to meet these challenges. They include the need for us to become more flexible, discerning, critical thinkers, and compassionate, caring and socially minded citizens. This is done by equipping us with the inner strength and qualities that enable us to make proactive and wise choices to influence and take an active part in decision making, have confidence, hope and optimism, and survive and even flourish in the face of rapidly moving social, technological and ecological developments.

However to rebalance the traditional preoccupations of traditional education, such as knowledge, technical skills and individual achievement and competition, with a greater emphasis on these personal and prosocial skills is not going to be easy. Educational attitudes, organisations and processes tend to lag behind rather than lead social change. Nor is it just a matter of proposing ever more content on top of an existing crowded curriculum. There is a need for a radical review of what education is about, what it is for how it can make better use of new modalities of learning and what its priorities should be. Within that review, we need to identify effective educational resources, approaches and tools that can accelerate the changes to hearts, minds, values and behaviour that are urgently needed.

POST-SCRIPT

What mindfulness contributes to educational and social transformation

Beyond the immediate priorities, a sister publication to this document, Mindfulness: developing agency in urgent times, outlines how mindfulness practice, and its underlying attitudes and values, can be the foundation and heart of an effort to steer humanity in a different direction and to make the radical shifts needed to tackle the crises that face humanity. [147] Mindfulness, including within education, can contribute the following fundamental perspectives, tools and values:

- a focus on the inner person, addressing and shifting the deep-seated impulses and habits that currently sustain the unsustainable.

- practical and embodied ways to cultivate new possibilities for the mind and heart, and developing transformative qualities and skills. These include a sense of power and agency reflection, attention regulation, receptivity, metacognition, a reduction in self-centeredness, cognitive flexibility, emotion regulation, sociability, and kindness.

- a focus on the essential ethics and values that can help move humanity forwards to a brighter and safer future, such as compassion, a sense of interconnection, open- mindedness, generosity, tolerance and altruism.

APPENDIX 1

Table of mindfulness programmes in the UK

Programmes currently available

Programme name, style, components	Materials and form of delivery	Target group	Training provided	Teacher pre-requisites	Cost	Research and evaluation, key findings, weblinks
Mindfulness in Schools Project https://mindfulnessinschools.org/ enquiries@mindfulnessinschools.org						
Paws b Classroom/ curriculum based, stand-alone mindfulness lessons. 'expertly crafted to teach a distinct mindfulness skill'. Based on content and principles of MBCT/MBSR adapted for children.	Scripts and materials for 12-lessons taught by classroom teachers or those working in youth-based contexts: slides, animations, exercises, worksheets and supporting materials.	11 years.	Teach Paws b 3 day training course. https://mindfulnessinschools.org/teach-paws-b/	Completed an 8-week mindfulness course (MBSR/ MBCT or equivalent) and have been practising mindfulness for at least 2-3 months.	£565 Supported places available	Vickery and Dorjee (2016) Controlled study of 9-year-olds (N= 71) from 3 UK primary school. Showed significant decreases in negative affect at follow-up, with a large effect size and small positive improvements in metacognition relative to controls. https://www.frontiersin.org/articles/10.3389/fpsyg.2015.02025/full
.b Classroom/ curriculum based, stand alone mindfulness lessons. 'expertly crafted to teach a distinct mindfulness skill'. Based on content and principles of MBCT/MBSR adapted for children.	Scripts and materials for 10 core lessons, and a further 8 'top-up' sessions. Taught by classroom teachers or those working in youth-based contexts: slides, animations, exercises, worksheets and supporting materials. Materials only available to those who have done the training.	11-13 years	Teach .b course 4-day training course. https://mindfulnessinschools.org/teach-dot-b/	Completed an 8-week mindfulness course (MBSR, MBCT or equivalent) and have been practising mindfulness for at least 2-3 months.	£760 Supported places available	Kuyken et al. (2013) Controlled study of 12 – 16-year olds (N = 522) in 12 secondary schools. Fewer depressive symptoms post-treatment and at follow-up and lower stress and greater wellbeing (P = 0.05) at follow-up relative to controls. More home practice associated with better outcomes. https://doi.org/10.1192/bjp.bp.113.126649
. breathe Combines SEL, mindfulness, neuroscience to introduce mindfulness as part of PSHE lessons and to support pre and post school transition.	4 scripted lessons, 30-60 mins taught once a week by classroom teachers. Classroom based, taught in PSHE/RSE curriculum or stand alone. Slides, animations, exercises, worksheets and supporting materials.	9-14 years	One day training	None - unlike the other MiSP programmes it's a taster of mindfulness alongside some SEL and neuroscience.. However, a commitment to engage in mindfulness practice during the course and ideally beyond is part of the Terms and Conditions for this course.	£195	No specific research on this programme. Originally part of Healthy Minds' PSHE curriculum programme for 11-14. Bounce Forward/ LSE partnership, funded by EEF. Small positive impacts on self-reported health measures smaller impacts on behavioural and emotional wellbeing measures. NB small increase in anxiety levels. http://eprints.lse.ac.uk/101236/1/Lordan_healthy_minds_the_positive_impact.pdf

TABLE OF MINDFULNESS PROGRAMMES IN THE UK

Programme name, style, components	Materials and form of delivery	Target group	Training provided	Teacher pre-requisites	Cost	Research and evaluation, key findings, weblinks
.b Foundations An 8-week introduction to mindfulness course offered within schools or other youth-related contexts for staff.	8 x 90 minute sessions and an Introductory session.	Teachers qualified to teach adult mindfulness course with a view to working in school settings.	3-day training	Recognised teacher training qualification mindfulness for adults. Taught 2 x 8 week courses (e.g. MBCT), Personal MFM practice.	£515	Beshai et al. (2015) CT of 89 secondary school staff, significant and large impacts on all outcome measures – increases in wellbeing, mindfulness and self-compassion, and decreases in stress. https://link.springer.com/article/10.1007%2Fs12671-015-0436-1
School mindfulness lead training To develop sustainable mindfulness in school, prep for leading .b foundations, become a 'mindfulness lead' within their organisation.	8 x 90 minute sessions and an Introductory session.	Must have trained to teach .b or Paws b curriculum and taught these courses at least twice. Must be employed by, or in long term relationship with, the school community in which .b Foundations will be taught to adults.	6.5 days residential training	.b and Paws b teachers.	Residential training is £1,265 no VAT. Online version is £895 over 12 days (some full days and some briefer practice session).	Evaluation of the .b Foundations programme, see above.
.begin Introduction to mindfulness for adults in the school community. Based on .b Foundations and MBCT/MBSR approach.	Live online training.	Teachers, school staff, educators, parents, volunteers and others in schools	8 x 90 minute sessions, face to face instructor-led, on line, connecting with a group.	No experience of mindfulness needed. Employed or volunteer in an educational setting or parent/carer of a child.	£150 for those in maintained schools. £195 + VAT otherwise.	See '.b Foundations'
dots https://mindfulnessinschools.org/teach-dots-3-6/dots-curriculum-ages-3-6/ The thirty sessions are designed to be flexible and varied and can be adapted to meet the needs of the children you are working with. Key themes explored sit alongside traditional MBSR/MBCT practices. Lead teacher is also trained to bring a 'support teacher' to offer some simple practices.	Materials to support 3 sets of 10 sessions – one set for each term. Sessions are taught by classroom teachers or those working in youth-based contexts: exercises, worksheets and detailed teacher support booklets	3-6 year-olds	Teach dots 3 day online training course. https://mindfulnessinschools.org/teach-dots-3-6/	Completed an 8-week mindfulness course (MBSR/ MBCT or equivalent) and have been practising mindfulness for at least 2-3 months.	£415 Supported places available	First offered in Spring 2021, so awaiting research
Teacher Development Programme A carousel of support and development CPD sessions for those who have trained to teach MiSP Curricula	Live online sessions involving practice, discussion and follow up links and resources	Those trained to teach Dots, .b, and Paws b	• Teaching Skills Workshops • Teaching Surgeries • Practice Sessions • Teachers' Retreats • One-to-one supervision • 'Inviting the Experts' webinars	Have completed training in any of the named MiSP curricula	Free to those who are active members of the MiSP trained teachers resource 'Hub'	N/A

TABLE OF MINDFULNESS PROGRAMMES IN THE UK

Programme name, style, components	Materials and form of delivery	Target group	Training provided	Teacher pre-requisites	Cost	Research and evaluation, key findings, weblinks

Youth Mindfulness
https://youthmindfulness.org/
info@youthmindfulness.org

Programme name, style, components	Materials and form of delivery	Target group	Training provided	Teacher pre-requisites	Cost	Research and evaluation, key findings, weblinks
The Kids Programme an in-depth introduction to mindfulness delivered by educators and classroom teachers. Drawing on positive psychology, MBSR and Plum Village/ Wake Up schools approach, the programme explores the cultivation of mindfulness, gratitude and kindness.	16 one-hour lessons over 8 weeks. Teaching materials only available to those who have done the training.	7-11 years	5-day training course.	Participants must have completed an 8-week mindfulness course (MBSR/MBCT or equivalent) and have been practising for at least 6 months.	£595	
SOMA programme - a flexible, responsive and trauma-informed mindfulness-based wellbeing programme for teens and young adults taking a discursive and group-learning approach to explore themes of mindfulness, character strengths, gratitude, kindness, agency and meaning and purpose.	Materials available to those who have done the course. Uses communication practices, team building games, the exploration of character strengths and values. Powerpoints, audio clips, videos, mini lectures.	12-21 years	5-day training course.	Participants must have completed an 8-week mindfulness course (MBSR/MBCT or equivalent) and have been practising mindfulness for at least 6 months.	£595	Simpson et al. (2019) Soma evaluated in prison setting. 25 qualitative interviews of incarcerated young men. Improvements in impulsivity, mental wellbeing, inner resilience, mindfulness, better sleep, less stress, feeling more in control, and improved relationships. https://link.springer.com/article/10.1007/s12671-018-1076-z
One year teacher training for mindfulness for life Cultivating key elements of mindfulness: embodiment, ease, joy and non-judgment.	Training centres on two retreats and 4 non-residential weekends. Self-study includes personal practice, reading, online content, meet in person or virtually with a peer group from within the training group. Practice one 'day of mindfulness' every two months alone or in local group.	Adults who want to teach mindfulness	2 x 5 day retreat plus 4 x 2 day non-residential	No pre-requisites other than a demonstrated intent to engage deeply with the programme learning and content.	£2,195 if paid in full in advance.	

The Goldie Hawn Foundation
https://mindup.org/

Programme name, style, components	Materials and form of delivery	Target group	Training provided	Teacher pre-requisites	Cost	Research and evaluation, key findings, weblinks
MindUP for Life Whole school SEL framework, training and curriculum 'to create a positive school wide culture and climate.' MindUP provides the knowledge and understanding of neuroscience, mindful awareness, positive psychology and daily practices to affect positive change both within the classroom and at home	An online curriculum of 15 lessons for teachers to implement in the classroom. The lessons are taught in sequence over the course of an academic year with mindful practices such as The Brain Break practiced 3x per day.	3-14 year olds	MindUP is available to receive virtual training as well as self paced training via an online platform. The online platform will be launching in Spring 2021 www.mindup.org The new MindUP for Life curriculum [2021] is available via online membership and training is available for individuals and schools, and school districts via self paced courses and/or virtual training provided by a certified MindUP consultant.	None	Virtual Training Costs will vary from c. £350 - £3000 per school based on the package the school selects. Online platform memberships will range from £35-£100 based on group size. Scholarships are available for those schools who need assistance	Summary and links to the papers at https://uk.mindup.org/research/ de Carvalho et al, (2017). Quasi-experimental study (N = 454) 8-9 year olds and 20 teachers. Significant increases in regulation of emotions, positive affect, and self-compassion, and decreased negative emotions. Improvements to teachers' wellbeing. Schonert-Reichl and Lawlor 2010) Control group design, 9-12-year olds (N= 246) Significant improvements on a wide range of (teacher-rated) aspects of social and emotional learning, such as aggression, behavioural dysregulation, and social competence, greater self-reported optimism and mindful attention. Schonert-Reichl et al, 2015) RCT (N=99) 9 -10 year olds. Significant increases in wide range of social and emotional skills, executive function, mindful attention, decreased depressive symptoms, enjoyment of school and gains in maths scores.

TABLE OF MINDFULNESS PROGRAMMES IN THE UK

Programme name, style, components	Materials and form of delivery	Target group	Training provided	Teacher pre-requisites	Cost	Research and evaluation, key findings, weblinks

The Present Courses CIC
info@thepresentcourses.org

Programme name, style, components	Materials and form of delivery	Target group	Training provided	Teacher pre-requisites	Cost	Research and evaluation, key findings, weblinks
The Present Course is an approach delivered by school staff weaving learning through everyday activities in school combining mindfulness and SEL, supporting learning across the curriculum, introduced over 14 weeks and offers an on-going structure to continue implementation.	Teaching manual for those who have done the course.	3-14 year olds	3-day training course plus implementation support for 12 months via Zoom meetings. Training is offered in a locality wherever possible to create a local team. Two free places in exchange for venue for training.	Completed an 8-week mindfulness course (MBSR/MBCT, The Present for Adults or equivalent) and have an established mindfulness practice.	£385–£495 depending on group size.	Small-scale interview-based study (N=8) with Key Stage 1 (3-7 year olds). Parents reported improvements in the children's emotional wellbeing. RCT with older primary school children currently under way in Vietnam. Data being collected before, after and 3 months follow up, will report Summer 2020. Included as an element of schools implementation in Iceland, currently being studied. Both described at http://thepresentcourses.org/?page_id=23

Mind With Heart
https://www.mindwithheart.org/
https://www.mindwithheart.org/contact-us

Programme name, style, components	Materials and form of delivery	Target group	Training provided	Teacher pre-requisites	Cost	Research and evaluation, key findings, weblinks
Connected teachers mindfulness and SEL tools for teachers own wellbeing and emotional health Care for ourselves Relax and find calm Develop self-awareness Build emotional intelligence Nourish healthy relationships	Materials available to those who take the course. These include participant booklet, access to video clips, slides, guided audios.	Teachers and educators	18 hours (9 x 2-hour sessions) Also online course 12 hours (8 x 1.5 hours).	Interest in mindfulness expected.	18 hours: £360 Online: £150	Hwang et al. (2019) Cluster RCT (N=185) educators in 20 schools received intervention to improve own wellbeing. Impacts in teachers on reduced perceived stress and sleep difficulty, increases in mindfulness, self-compassion, and cognitive reappraisal in emotion regulation. Medium to large effect sizes, post intervention and 6-weeks later. Improved educator wellbeing impacted on students' sense of connectedness to teachers, without any interventions for students. https://link.springer.com/article/10.1007/s12671-019-01147-1
Connected with Myself Explores tools for teaching teens to have more attention, resilience, metacognition, self-care and emotional health. Includes neuroscience, empathy and compassion exercises, debates, games, perspective taking, and understanding the mind.	Materials available to those who take the course. These include participant booklet, access to video clips, slides, guided audios.	Teachers of 11-18 year olds	3 day training course (18 hours)	Familiarity with mindfulness.	£360	Qualitative study undertaken by researcher at Montpellier University, publication forthcoming.
Connected With Others Explores tools for mindfulness, compassion and SEL and how these can be presented to teenagers to enhance self-care, motivation and pro-social behaviour.	Materials available to those who take the training. These include participant booklet, access to video clips, slides, guided audios.	Teachers of 11-18 year olds	3 day training course (18 hours)	Familiarity expected with SEL.	£360	Qualitative study undertaken by MA student at the Institute of Education, UCL.

TABLE OF MINDFULNESS PROGRAMMES IN THE UK

Programme name, style, components	Materials and form of delivery	Target group	Training provided	Teacher pre-requisites	Cost	Research and evaluation, key findings, weblinks
Jigsaw - the mindful approach to PSHE https://www.jigsawpshe.com/ office@janlevergroup.com						
Jigsaw Teaching and Learning Programme includes elements of mindfulness within a PSHE/RSE programme in a spiral, progressive scheme of work. Elements of mindfulness include awareness of thoughts and emotions, concentration, focus and visualisation.	Teaching Programmes can be bought from the Jigsaw website	Teachers of 3-11 and 11-16 year olds	Schools buy the curriculum materials and receive free on-going mentor and online support with free updates. Additional training and support at additional cost.	None	Primary whole school set of materials £1995 + VAT (& delivery) Secondary whole school set of materials £1450 + VAT	Qualitative study published by the programme, undertaken by Sheffield Hallam Uni, suggested acceptability and perceived usefulness of the PSHE programme by 195 teachers in 101 schools, and measured the impact on 812 children's emotional literacy using a standardised emotional literacy assessment tool. The mindfulness component was not evaluated separately from the overall PSHE programme. https://www.jigsawpshe.com/does-jigsaw-work/
Wake Up Schools Plum Village, France https://wakeupschools.org/ info@wakeupschools.org						
Wake Up Schools Two levels of training through week long Educators' Retreats and mentoring. Supported by weekends and days of mindfulness for educators and other resources e.g. guidebook, film and materials for young people, generic retreats.	Two levels of teacher training. Guidebook and books for young people can be bought on the web.	Teachers and other educators Books and materials for young people	Teacher training Level I: Taking Care of the Teacher- retreat based. Run in many countries including the UK. Level 2 Teaching Mindfulness and Applied Ethics to Students a year long mentorship relationship with an experienced Plum Village Mindfulness Teacher.	TT level 1 for anyone. TT level 2 attended a Plum Village retreat or Wake Up Schools Level I Training, and regular practice with mindfulness community	Retreat prices vary according to individual accommodation choices. €350 is average for a week's retreat, food, accommodation and teachings.	Qualitative case studies and testimonies in the guidebook 'Happy Teachers Change the World: a guide to cultivating mindfulness through education' and film 'Happy teachers will change the world' – see website.

Programmes currently under development

Programme name, style, components	Materials and form of delivery	Target group	Training provided	Teacher pre-requisites	Cost	Research and evaluation, key findings, weblinks
Compassion in Schools www.cmtschools.org University of Derby/Compassionate Mind Foundation/ University of Coimbra, Portugal						
Compassionate mind training (CMT) via 6 modules covering: • Definition of compassion • Exploration of emotions and the stress response • Building the compassionate mind. • Using the compassionate mind to address stress • Using the compassionate mind to address problems of self-criticism. • Compassion & compassionate flows: a whole school ethos/ use in everyday life.	The 6 modules are delivered with a combination of teaching, videos and live contemplative/ experiential practices. These include core mindfulness practices to enable observation of the contents of the mind as they arise and to allow improved emotional and behavioural regulation.	Teachers, educators and those working in education (i.e. whole school ethos) in the first instance. Pupil curricular for 8-10 and 11-15 in development	Run over 1 school term, with 1.5 hour modules bi-weekly to fit into staff CPD allocation.	No prerequisites & all staff invited to take part.	Provided from a research grant. Cost of training in curriculum delivery TBC	Maratos et al., (2019). Feasibility study with >70 educators revealed many benefits of CMT to counteract the current competition-based nature of education, especially the stresses contributing to negative changes in wellbeing. https://link.springer.com/article/10.1007/s12671-019-01185-9 Several further papers are in preparation and the number of educators who have received the programme now exceeds 500. For more information see: www.cmtschools.org www.compassionatemind.co.uk

APPENDIX 2

Systematic reviews and meta-analyses of Mindfulness Based Interventions for teachers and school aged youth

Mindfulness for teachers

Zarate, K. Maggin, D. and Passmore, A. (2019) *Meta-analysis of mindfulness training on teacher well-being Psychology in Schools Volume 56*, Issue10 1700-1715

> 18 manuscripts that included a total sample of 1,001 educators. Mindfulness interventions ranged greatly in dosage, frequency, and delivery model. Using a random effects model, mindfulness-based interventions were found to have significant positive effects across all domains. Mindfulness-based interventions resulted in large effects on feelings of mindfulness, moderate effects for decreases in stress and anxiety, and small effects on feelings of depression and burnout.

Klingbeil, D.and Renshaw, T. (2018) *Mindfulness-Based Interventions for Teachers: A Meta-Analysis of the Emerging Evidence Base School Psychology Quarterly 33*, (4) 501–511
http://dx.doi.org/10.1037/spq0000291

> Included 29 studies. MBIs had a medium treatment effect on teacher outcomes MBIs were associated with small-to-medium positive effects on therapeutic processes and therapeutic outcomes. MBIs had the smallest effects on measures of classroom climate and instructional practices.

Hwang, Y., Bartlett, B. Greben, M., and Hand, K. (2017) *A Systematic Review of Mindfulness Interventions for In-Service Teachers: A tool to enhance teacher wellbeing and performance. Teaching and Teacher Education.* 64, 26-42.

> Sixteen studies published up to 2015. Looked at research and intervention design, interventionists, intervention results, intervention fidelity, and measurement validity and reliability. Interventions were provided primarily to enhance teacher wellbeing and teacher performance, both were enhanced by mindfulness, especially wellbeing.

Emerson, L-M, Leyland, A, Hudson, K et al. (3 more authors) (2017) *Teaching Mindfulness to Teachers: A Systematic Review and Narrative Synthesis. Mindfulness, 8* (5). pp. 1136-1149. ISSN 1868-8527

> A systematic based on 13 studies. As would be expected in a new area, MBIs did not show uniform results, but significant impacts were shown across the studies on anxiety and depression, burnout, stress, physical symptoms, sleep, time pressure, sense of accomplishment and satisfaction with life. The authors hypothesised that improved emotion regulation lay behind these shifts.

Lomas, T. et al. (2017) *The impact of mindfulness on the wellbeing and performance of educators: A Systematic Review of the Empirical Literature. Teaching and Teacher Education.*

> A total of 19 papers met the eligibility criteria and were included in the systematic review, consisting of a total 1981 participants. Studies were principally examined for outcomes such as burnout, anxiety, depression and stress, as well as more positive wellbeing measures (e.g., life satisfaction). The systematic review revealed that mindfulness was generally associated with positive outcomes in relation to most measures.

Mindfulness with School Aged Youth

McKeering. P. and Hwang, Y. (2019) *A systematic review of mindfulness-based school interventions with early adolescents.* Mindfulness 10:593–610 https://doi.org/10.1007/s12671-018-0998-9

> A search carried out in nine electronic databases resulted in an initial selection of 1571 records, from which 13 papers emerged that met all inclusion criteria (the search was restricted to 11-14 year olds). The review found positive improvements reported in wellbeing measures in 11 of the 13 papers examined across both quantitative and qualitative data that provide support for mindfulness as a wellbeing school preventative program with this age group.

Mak, C., Whittingham, K., Cunnington, R. et al. (2018) *Efficacy of Mindfulness-Based Interventions for Attention and Executive Function in Children and Adolescents—A Systematic Review. Mindfulness* 9, 59–78 https://doi.org/10.1007/s12671-017-0770-6

> A systematic review of 13 RCTs of mindfulness (7) and of yoga (3). Studies recruited adolescents or children that were typically developing, diagnosed with attention-deficit hyperactivity disorder, orphans, or had reading difficulties, or in correctional schools/institutions. The quality of the 13 studies ranged from low to high. Five of the 13 studies found a statistically significant intervention effect for at least one outcome measure of attention or executive function with medium to large effect sizes (0.3–32.03). The review concluded that mindfulness based interventions are a promising approach to targeting attention and executive function in children and adolescence.

Dunning. D.L., Griffiths, K., Kuyken, W., Crane, C., Foulkes, L., Parker, J., & Dalgleish, T. (2018). *The Effects of Mindfulness Based Interventions on Cognition and Mental Health in Children and Adolescents - A Meta-Analysis of Randomized Controlled Trials. Journal of Child Psychology and Psychiatry.* 60(3):244-258

> A systematic literature search of RCTs of MBIs produced 33 studies. Across all RCTs the authors found significant positive effects of MBIs, relative to controls, for mindfulness, self-regulation, executive function, attention, depression, anxiety/stress and negative behaviours, with small effect sizes. However, when considering only those RCTs with active control groups, significant benefits of an MBI were restricted to the outcomes of mindfulness, depression, and anxiety/stress.

Black, D. S. (2016). '*Mindfulness Training for Children and Adolescents: A state-of-the-science review*'. In K. W. Brown, J. D. Creswell, and R. M. Ryan (Eds.), Handbook of Mindfulness: Theory, Research, and Practice. Guilford: New York, NY.

> Systematically reviewed 41 MBI studies, including 13 RCTs, conducted in school and clinical settings. They concluded that MBIs in schools reliably impact on a wide range of indicators of wellbeing including: aspects of cognition and self-regulation, particularly the ability to pay attention; psycho-social variables such as emotional regulation, interpersonal relationships, stress, depression and anxiety; and measures of psycho-biological outcomes such as blood pressure and heart rate.

Zenner, C., Herrnleben-Kurz, S., and Walach, H. *Mindfulness-Based Interventions in Schools—A systematic Review and Meta-Analysis.* Frontiers in Psychology. 5:603: 1-20. doi: 10.3389/fpsyg.2014.00603. 2014.

> This is a systematic review of MBIs in schools, enhanced by the inclusion of a meta-analysis of 24 MBIs, exploring a wide range of psycho-social and cognitive domains. It found a significant medium effect size across all controlled studies, with strongest effects in the domain of cognitive performance.

Felver, J. C., Doerner, E., Jones, J., Kaye, N. C. and Merrell, K. W. (2015) *Mindfulness in School Psychology: Applications for Intervention and Professional Practice; Psychology in Schools*, 50: 531–547. doi:10.1002/pits.21695

> A systematic review of studies in school settings, with a helpful commentary on the field. It concluded from 28 studies, including 10 RCTs, that MBIs can be effective at reducing '*psychosocial problems and supporting positive attributes*' (in which they included mental health indicators, social and emotional learning, cognitive function and physiological measures).

Zoogman, S., Goldberg, S. B., Hoyt, W. T. and Miller, L. (2014) *Mindfulness Interventions With Youth: A Meta-Analysis. Mindfulness,* 6(2), 290-302

> A meta-analysis of mindfulness interventions with youth aged 6–21 years (including non-school settings) identified 20 studies that met its criteria. It found MBIs showed effect sizes in the small to moderate range for all outcomes, including emotion and behavioral regulation, depressive and anxiety symptoms, stress, attention, and cognitive functioning.

Kallapiran, K., Koo, S., Kirubakaran, R., and Hancock, K. (2015) *Effectiveness of Mindfulness in Improving Mental Health Symptoms of Children and Adolescents: A meta-analysis.* Child and Adolescent Mental Health, 20: 182–194.

    A meta-analysis analysed 11 RCTs which targeted mental health outcomes in both clinical and non-clinical samples of young people ranging from 6 to 18 years old. It concluded that MBIs with non-clinical samples (including schools) had small effects on stress and depression, and large effects on anxiety.

Maynard, B.R., Solis, M.R., Miller, V.L., and Brendel, K. E. (2017) *Mindfulness-based Interventions for Improving Cognition, Academic Achievement, Behaviour, and Socio-Emotional Functioning of Primary and Secondary School Students.* Campbell Systematic Reviews:5. DOI: 10.4073/csr2017.5.

    A systematic review and meta-analysis of MBIs for school aged children in a range of settings, which identified 61 studies for systematic review, and 35 randomized or quasi-experimental studies for further meta-analysis. It found small positive effects on cognitive and socioemotional outcomes, and positive but non-significant effects on academic and behavioral outcomes. The authors did not find enough studies to estimate the size of impacts on physiological measures of health.

Klingbeil, D.A., Renshaw, T.L., Willenbrink, J.B., Copek, R.A., Chan, K., Haddock, and Clifton, J. (2017) *Mindfulness-Based Interventions With Youth: A Comprehensive Meta-Analysis of Group Design Studies.* Journal of School Psychology. 63: 77-103. .

    A meta-analysis of 76 studies in a range of youth related settings. It concluded that MBIs yield a small positive average treatment effect across all outcomes, with the largest effect being seen academic achievement and school functioning, and slightly lower but still positive effects on metacognition, attention, cognitive flexibility, emotional/behavioral regulation, mental health issues/ internalizing problems (e.g. distress, depression and anxiety), positive emotions and self-appraisal. It reported larger effect sizes at follow up than immediately after interventions.

APPENDIX 3

Outcome measures often used in evaluating the impact of Mindfulness Based Interventions in school contexts

Building on section 3 on the evidence base, this is a list of the most frequently used tools and measures that have been used in research on mindfulness in schools, with students and teachers. It focuses wherever possible on measures used in recent UK studies. Many of these measures have separate versions for children and for adults. Almost all listed here are free to download and use for schools, although some need the researcher to give details and request a license. Some measures allow the items to be adapted, but some do not allow this under their rules of copyright.

Mindfulness

Five Facet Mindfulness Questionnaire (FFMQ)
The measure most often used with adults, 39 items measuring five aspects of mindfulness. There is a shorter 15 item version which has also been shown to be reasonably valid and reliable.

- https://positivepsychology.com/five-facet-mindfulness-questionnaire-ffmq/

- http://ruthbaer.com/academics/FFMQ.pdf

- Baer, R. A., Hopkins, J., Krietemeyer, J., Smith, G. T., & Toney, L. (2006). Using Self-Report Assessment Methods to Explore Facets of Mindfulness Assessment, 13(1), 27-45.

The Mindfulness in Teaching Scale
A 14-item scale designed specifically for teachers which measures interpersonal mindfulness as well as intrapersonal (self) mindfulness.

- https://www.researchgate.net/publication/289250326_Validation_of_the_Mindfulness_in_Teaching_Scale

- Frank, Jennifer & Jennings, Patricia & Greenberg, Mark. (2015). Validation of the Mindfulness in Teaching Scale. Mindfulness. 7. 10

Child Adolescent Mindfulness Measure (CAMM)
This 10-item measure was developed specifically for children and young people and is suitable for ages 10-17.

- https://educationendowmentfoundation.org.uk/projects-and-evaluation/evaluating-projects/measuring-essential-skills/spectrum-database/child-and-adolescent-mindfulness-measure/

- Greco, L. A., Baer, R. A., & Smith, G. T. (2011). Assessing mindfulness in children and adolescents: development and validation of the Child and Adolescent Mindfulness Measure (CAMM). Psychological Assessment, 23(3), 606-614. doi:10.1037/a0022819

- Kuby, A. K., McLean, N., & Allen, K. (2015). Validation of the Child and Adolescent Mindfulness Measure (CAMM) with Non-Clinical Adolescents. Mindfulness, 6(6), 1448-1455. doi:10.1007/s12671-015-0418-3

OUTCOME MEASURES OFTEN USED IN EVALUATING THE IMPACT OF MBIS IN SCHOOL CONTEXTS

Psycho-social outcomes

Toolkit to evaluate mental health and wellbeing
- An overlapping list of 30 tools used to measure aspects of mental health and wellbeing has been produced by Public Health England with the Anna Freud Centre and can be found at https://www.annafreud.org/media/4612/mwb-toolki-final-draft-4.pdf

What follows here are the ones most often used in evaluating mindfulness interventions.

Warwick Edinburgh Mental Wellbeing Scale
(WEMWEBS) Age range 13 upwards. Widely used with teens and adults. Full version is 14 items, shortened form is several.

- https://warwick.ac.uk/fac/sci/med/research/platform/wemwbs

- Research using WEMWEBS https://warwick.ac.uk/fac/sci/med/research/platform/wemwbs/research/research/

Stirling Children's Wellbeing Scale
Ages 8-15. 15 items measuring optimism, cheerfulness and relaxation, satisfying interpersonal relationships, positive functioning including clear thinking and competence

https://czone.eastsussex.gov.uk/media/4891/the-stirling-childrens-wellbeing-scale.pdf

- Ian Liddle & Greg F.A. Carter (2015) Emotional and psychological well-being in children: the development and validation of the Stirling Children's Well-being Scale, Educational Psychology in Practice, 31:2, 174-185, DOI: 10.1080/02667363.2015.1008409 https://www.tandfonline.com/doi/abs/10.1080/02667363.2015.1008409

The Good Childhood Index. https://www.childrenssociety.org.uk/what-we-do/research/well-being/background-programme/good-childhood-index

An index of subjective wellbeing for children aged eight and over developed by the Children's Society, it includes a single-item measure of happiness with life as a whole, a five-item measure of overall life satisfaction, and questions about ten different aspects of life including happiness with school life and relationships with family and friends. It is used by the Society for their annual report, and can be used by schools by e-mailing the Society, and is free to use provided acknowledgement of the source is made.

Strengths and Difficulties Questionnaire (SDQ).
Extremely widely used across research with the young. 25 items ask about emotions, relations with others and behaviour. Versions for adults to complete for 2-16, self-completion versions for 11-17, and for over 18, plus versions for low or high risk populations.

- https://www.sdqinfo.org/

Maslach Burnout Inventory for educators
The original burnout inventory was developed over 35 years, this is the version for educators. Measures emotional exhaustion, depersonalisation (acting numbly) and sense of personal accomplishment at work. There are costs to use, but they are reasonable, and a manual with guidance and individual or group analysis are offered.

- https://www.mindgarden.com/316-mbi-educators-survey

Perceived Stress Scale (PSS)
For adults and The Perceived Stress Scale - Children (PSS-C) for 5-18 years. The most widely used tools to assess stress. Measures the degree to which situations are seen and appraised as stressful. Items are designed to tap how unpredictable, uncontrollable, and overloaded respondents find their lives over the last month. The scale also includes a number of direct queries about current levels of experienced stress.

- http://www.mindgarden.com/documents/PerceivedStressScale.pdf

- https://www.bouncetogether.co.uk/resources/perceived-stress-scale-children

Center for Epidemiological Studies Depression Scale (CES-D) and **Center for Epidemiologic Studies Depression Scale for Children (CES-C).**
This widely used tool measures depressive thinking and behaviour. It asks about experience of a range of symptoms related to depression in the last week.

- https://www.midss.org/content/center-epidemiologic-studies-depression-scale-ces-d

- Radloff, L.S. (1977) The CES-D scale: A self report depression scale for research in the general population. Applied Psychological Measurement 1: 385-401.

- **Centre for Epidemiological Studies Depression Scale for Children (CES-DC)** https://www.psychtools.info/cesdc/

Revised Children's Anxiety and Depression Scale (RCADS) Measures anxiety in particular and asks young people aged 8-18 how often they experience a whole range of symptoms associated with anxiety. There is also a version for adults to complete about children.

- https://novopsych.com.au/assessments/revised-child-anxiety-and-depression-scale-child-rcads-child/
- https://www.corc.uk.net/outcome-experience-measures/revised-childrens-anxiety-and-depression-scale-and-subscales/

Positive and Negative Affect Schedule (PANAS)
Is a self-report scale that consists of different words that describe feelings and emotions, one scale measures positive affect (emotions) and the other negative. Long, short, adult and children's versions (PANAS C) have been developed. The children's one takes about 5 minutes to complete.

- https://positivepsychology.com/positive-and-negative-affect-schedule-panas/

Self-Compassion Scale (SCS).
In the long form for adults, six constructs are measured across 26 items: self-kindness, common humanity, and mindfulness and their negative opposite constructs of self-judgment, isolation, and over-identification. There is a shorter 12 item version for adults, and versions for children and for teenagers.

- https://positivepsychology.com/self-compassion-scale/

The Emotion Regulation Questionnaire
10 items designed to assess individual differences in the habitual use of two emotion regulation strategies: cognitive reappraisal and expressive suppression.

- https://www.ocf.berkeley.edu/~johnlab/pdfs/ERQ.pdf
- Gross, J.J., & John, O.P. (2003). Individual differences in two emotion regulation processes: Implications for affect, relationships, and well-being. Journal of Personality and Social Psychology, 85, 348-362.

Teachers' Sense of Efficacy Scale
Long form 24 items, short form 12. Measures how effective teachers believe they are at tasks involved in running a classroom and relating to students.

- https://vulms.vu.edu.pk/Courses/PSY406/Downloads/Teacher%20Self-Efficacy%20Sclae.pdf
- https://www.statisticssolutions.com/teacher-self-efficacy-scale

Social and emotional learning

SEL is a vast field with many components and thus many different measures of them. At the moment there is no front runner. National bodies in the UK and the US have so far come up with guidance on assessing the field, and some tables of different measures that schools might consider, depending on what they want to know.

SPECTRUM (Social, Psychological, Emotional, Concepts of self, and Resilience: Understanding and Measurement)

This is a project from the Education Endowment Fund.

- It reviews the issues on measuring the field https://educationendowmentfoundation.org.uk/projects-and-evaluation/evaluating-projects/measuring-essential-skills/
- It has a table of 84 measures of various dimensions, compared with one another. https://educationendowmentfoundation.org.uk/projects-and-evaluation/evaluating-projects/measuring-essential-skills/spectrum-database/

SEL Assessment Guide (SAG)
The SAG has been produced in the US by The Collaborative for Academic, Social, and Emotional Learning (CASEL) who are the world leading authorities on SEL. The SAG is an interactive tool to help practitioners select and effectively use currently available assessments of students' SEL competencies. It includes links to many different measures as well as valuable advice on the whole issue.

- https://measuringsel.casel.org/assessment-guide/

School climate

The Comprehensive School Climate Inventory (CSCI) is a nationally-recognised school climate survey from the US. It has recently been used by the UK's MYRIAD project on mindfulness in the UK after a systematic trawl of all the available instruments on school climate. It provides a profile of a school community's strengths, as well as areas for improvement. Different versions can be completed by students, parents / guardians, and school personnel. For a copy of the full scales (the website has samples only) and for permission to use, contact the email on the website.

- https://www.schoolclimate.org/services/measuring-school-climate-csci

OUTCOME MEASURES OFTEN USED IN EVALUATING THE IMPACT OF MBIS IN SCHOOL CONTEXTS

Physiological measures

It is not likely that a school on its own will make much use of physiological measures as this will involve an ethics committee, and certainly permission from parents in the case of the children. However, the development of wearable technological devices which include some physiological/behavioural indices, such as heart rate, have made some physiological measures more possible and less intrusive. Below is a selection of some common physiological aspects that have proved to be affected by mindfulness.

- Heart rate
- Blood pressure
- Sleep quality
- Cortisol levels

APPENDIX 4

Useful websites and apps

Mindfulness

https://www.themindfulnessinitiative.org/ – The Mindfulness Initiative was founded in 2013 and believes that capacities of heart and mind should be central to public policy making. On the site you'll find publications promoting the use of mindfulness in policy areas such as education, health, criminal justice, the workplace and politics.

www.Mindful.org is a US site and popular resource for the general public. It includes guidance on getting started with a mindfulness practice and articles about the science of mindfulness and mindfulness-based programmes.

UK mindfulness university research centres:

https://www.bangor.ac.uk/mindfulness/ – The Centre for Mindfulness Research and Practice (CMRP) was the first university-based mindfulness centre in the UK. They run mindfulness teacher-training courses, including a Masters in Mindfulness, as well as publishing research into the impact on mindfulness.

https://www.oxfordmindfulness.org/ – the University of Oxford Mindfulness Centre has a website for the general public and it offers mindfulness classes online and in person. They run free weekly mindfulness sessions and the site allows you to keep up to date with the latest research.

http://myriadproject.org/ – The MYRIAD Project (My Resilience in Adolescence) is a collaboration between the universities of Oxford, Cambridge, University College London, Exeter and others. With around 540 schools involved and over 35,000 students at baseline, it is investigating whether a mindfulness-based intervention is effective and cost-effective when compared with normal classroom teaching.

https://www.exeter.ac.uk/mooddisorders/networks/exetermindfulnessnetwork/ – Through cultivating mindfulness, the Exeter Mindfulness Centre has the intention to reduce human suffering, promote wellbeing and create the conditions in which people can flourish.

Mindfulness teachers and courses

https://bamba.org.uk/ – The British Association of Mindfulness-based Approaches exists to support and develop good practice and integrity in the delivery of mindfulness-based approaches. On the site there is a directory to find mindfulness teachers in your area, 'Good Practice Guidelines', and other resources to support people's understanding of mindfulness.

https://www.accessmbct.com/ – Mindfulness-based Cognitive Therapy is recommended by the NHS for people who suffer from recurrent depression. You can find an MBCT teacher via the international directory listed on this website.

https://www.bemindfulonline.com/ – Approved by the NHS, this is the only Mindfulness-Based Cognitive Therapy (MBCT) course available online. The course is a 4-week, learn at your own pace, MBCT digital programme.

https://palousemindfulness.com/ – a completely free 8-week Mindfulness-Based Stress Reduction (MBSR) course, based on the programme founded by Jon Kabat-Zinn.

Wellbeing research

https://whatworkswellbeing.org/ – The What Works Centre for Wellbeing is an independent centre that develops and shares robust and accessible evidence to show what impacts on wellbeing in society. They have articles and resources on improving wellbeing in areas such as education, and children and young people.

https://ggsc.berkeley.edu/ – Based at the University of California Berkeley, the Greater Good Science Center provides a bridge between the research community

USEFUL WEBSITES AND APPS

and the general public. The website shares articles and resources from the 'science of wellbeing' with mindfulness featuring heavily.

Research and practice in mindfulness, contemplative approaches and SEL

https://www.mindandlife-europe.org/mle-initiatives/education-cce/ – Mind and Life Europe Community of Contemplative Education (CCE) set up in 2018 develops the theory and practice of contemplative and mindfulness-based education in Europe, in schools and universities. Its website is aimed at the public, and includes links to a database of programmes to be found across Europe, reports on the outcomes of meetings and consultations, and links to videos and presentations made especially for the CCE, and to the research and publications of its expert members, including some from the UK such as Katherine Weare, co-author of this guidance, and Guy Claxton and Dusana Dorjee who contributed to it.

https://educationendowmentfoundation.org.uk/ – The Education Endowment Foundation is a charity dedicated to breaking the link between family income and educational achievement. The website contains summaries of the best available evidence for raising attainment in schools in plain language for busy, time-poor teachers and senior leaders.

https://casel.org/ – The Collaborative for Academic, Social, and Emotional Learning (CASEL) share research, resources and information about high-quality, evidence-based social and emotional learning (SEL – in which they include mindfulness) including detailed support with implementation. They have been developing for many decades, and their website is a rich resource.

Apps

https://www.headspace.com/educators – a very popular mindfulness app with engaging videos and a wide variety of meditations. Headspace have offered their app for free for UK educators.

https://insighttimer.com/ – another popular app that can be used for free (as well as a paid subscription) and has guided meditations recorded by respected contemplatives such as Matthieu Ricard and Jack Kornfield, and 'celebrity' meditators such as Goldie Hawn, and Russell Brand.

https://www.smilingmind.com.au/ – a free mindfulness app for schools and students from Australia, designed by psychologists and educators.

Measuring wellbeing in schools

https://www.corc.uk.net/resource-hub/wellbeing-measurement-framework-wmf/ – The Child Outcomes Research Consortium (CORC), along with other partners, created this wellbeing measurement toolkit for schools, with guidance and validated measures to use.

https://www.corc.uk.net/eLearning/ – a free and useful e-learning module developed by CORC on 'Measuring mental wellbeing to improve the lives of children and young people'.

https://whatworkswellbeing.org/blog/measuring-wellbeing-in-schools-and-colleges/ – a blog written by the Mindfulness Initiative's Education Policy Co-Lead, Adrian Bethune, about the benefits and difficulties of measuring wellbeing in schools.

Videos and TED Talks about mindfulness

https://www.ted.com/talks/andy_puddicombe_all_it_takes_is_10_mindful_minutes – **All It Takes is 10 Mindful Minutes** by Andy Puddicombe, the co-founder of Headspace.

https://www.ted.com/talks/matthieu_ricard_how_to_let_altruism_be_your_guide – **How To Let Altruism Be Your Guide**. Matthieu Ricard, a happiness researcher and a Buddhist monk, argues altruism is a great lens for making decisions, both for the short and long term, in work and in life.

https://www.ted.com/talks/matt_killingsworth_want_to_be_happier_stay_in_the_moment#t-139046 – **Want To Be Happier? Stay In The Moment.** Matt Killingsworth built an app, Track Your Happiness, that let people report their feelings in real time. Among the surprising results: We're often happiest when we're lost in the moment. And the flip side: The more our mind wanders, the less happy we can be.

https://www.youtube.com/watch?v=6mlk6xD_xAQ&t=526s – **Mindfulness in Schools.** In this talk co-founder of the Mindfulness in Schools Project, Richard Burnett, guides the audience through a short mindfulness meditation suitable as an initial practice with young people, and shares his experience of teaching mindfulness in schools.

APPENDIX 5

Further reading

Schonert-Reichl, Kimberly A., and Roeser, Robert W (eds). *Handbook of Mindfulness in Education: Integrating Theory and Research Into Practice.* New York: Springer, 2016.

    This substantial reader is the first attempt at providing a comprehensive and authoritative summary of a wide range of work on mindfulness and contemplative approaches, set mainly in the United States. Edited by two leading lights who are also authors, and with 22 papers written by other leaders of the field, it summarises the state of the science and describes current and emerging applications and challenges, integrating history, theory, philosophy, research, practice, and policy.

Hawkins, Kevin. *Mindful Teacher, Mindful School.* Sage, London. 2017.

    Written by an ex head teacher and one time director of the international arm of the UK Mindfulness in Schools project, this very accessible book provides practical guidance on how to implement mindfulness across the stressful and busy lives of teachers and the entirety of the school, as well as into classroom teaching. Anecdotes taken from work in many countries give it plenty of colour.

Nhat Hanh, Thich, and Weare, Katherine. *Happy Teachers Change the World: A guide to cultivating mindfulness in education.* San Francisco: Parallax, 2017.

    This is the first guidebook to the influential teaching of world respected Zen master and seminal writer and practitioner on mindfulness, Thich Nhat Hanh. It synthesizes his teachings with instructions for core practices from the Plum Village tradition, educational guidance on how to apply these practices of mindfulness, kindness and compassion in one's own life, and in classrooms, schools and universities, illustrated with first hand examples from the practice of teachers from around the world.

Willard, Christopher, and Saltzman, Amy. *Teaching Mindfulness Skills to Kids and Teens.* New York: the Guilford Press, 2015.

    Starting with a succinct chapter on well documented current research findings, the main thrust of this book is practical. It aims to impart creative, effective ideas for bringing mindfulness into the classroom, child therapy office, and community. It features sample lesson plans and scripts, case studies, and vignettes, and explores strategies for overcoming obstacles, engaging the young and integrating mindfulness into a broad range of activities. The main examples are from the US.

Jennings, Patricia, Mindfulness for Teachers: *Simple Skills for Peace and Productivity in the Classroom.* New York: Norton. 2015

    This US guidebook is written by a mindfulness expert who combines an academic base and solid research experience in neuroscience, psychology, and education with applied mindfulness teaching and programme development. The book focuses mainly on the teacher's own mindfulness, suggesting the principles for managing classroom stresses, cultivating the learning environment and applying mindfulness in classrooms.

Brown, Valerie and Olson, Kirsten. *The Mindful School Leader.* Thousand Oaks, CA: Sage 2015

    The only book to date aimed at school leaders and written by two leading US school leadership trainers, this handbook outlines techniques for adding mindfulness into daily school life, including managing meetings and responding creatively to complex situations. It includes profiles of real life mindful school leaders and a guide to resources including apps.

CORE READING

Schoeberlein David, Deborah and Seth, Suki. *Mindful Teaching and Teaching Mindfulness: A Guide for Anyone Who Teaches Anything.* Somerville Massachusetts: Wisdom Publications, 2009.

This very practical, straightforward and easy to read book from the US, aimed at 'teachers' of all kinds, including parents and coaches, follows a school teacher through their day, focusing on how teachers can tune into what's happening, inside and around them to plant the seed for an education infused with attention, awareness, kindness, empathy, compassion, and gratitude.

Rotne, Kikolaj and Rotne, Didde Flor. *Everybody Present.* Berkley: Parallax. 2009.

This reflective 'working manual' by Danish educators reframes the culture of education and student-teacher relationship, illustrating the transformative effects of mindfulness on educators, students, and their classrooms. With stories, exercises, and case studies it suggests that mindfulness can help to strengthen inner peace and prevent stress, foster contagious joy and an ethic of altruism, and improve understanding and relationships.

Olsen, Kirke and Cozolino, Louis. *The Invisible Classroom: Relationships, Neuroscience and Mindfulness in School.* New York: Norton, 2014.

A thoughtful synthesis of brain science, mindfulness, and positive psychology, based on the premise that all classroom interactions have 'invisible' neurobiological, emotional, and social aspects, including the emotional histories of students, and the teacher's own background and biography, which the teacher needs to grasp to understand the full range of their students' school experiences. It includes classroom-ready resources to help practitioners turn these insights into practice.

Kaiser Greenland, Susan. *The Mindful Child.* New York: Atrea/Simon and Schuster, 2013.

This highly influential book is written for educators and parents by the founder of the positively evaluated US Inner Kids programme and is based on her extensive experience of teaching mindfulness to children, including cultivating kindness and compassion. It has an accessible, homely style and is particularly strong on practical tips, caveats and examples from life. It is mainly focused on younger age groups.

Srinivasan, Meena. *Teach, Breathe, Learn: Mindfulness in and out of the Classroom.* Berkley, California: Parallax, 2009.

A highly practical book, written by a classroom teacher and based on her own experience, inspired by a range of influences, most evidently the work of Thich Nhat Hanh and Plum Village. Part one focuses on the teacher's own mindfulness, part two offers techniques for cultivating loving-kindness, gratitude and empathy, and part three introduces a curriculum that teachers can use to incorporate mindfulness into their classroom, with lesson plans, handouts, and homework assignments.

Nhat Hanh, Thich. *Planting Seeds.* Berkley: Parallax, 2009.

Based on Thich Nhat Hanh's thirty years of practical experience teaching mindfulness and compassion to parents, teachers, and children, the book and CD offer insight, concrete activities, and curricula that parents and educators can apply in school settings, in their local communities or at home in working with children, aged from 5-11. The CD has recordings of all the songs in the book as well as instructions for meditations. The book is pleasantly and simply illustrated.

Broderick, Patricia C. *Learning to Breathe: A Mindfulness Curriculum for Adolescents to Cultivate Emotional Regulation, Attention and Performance.* Oakland: New Harbinger, 2013.

The comprehensive and clear manual for the evaluated US 'Learning to Breathe' curriculum. It begins with a succinct account of the research base for mindfulness and the wider work of SEL and is thereafter a step by step guide to teaching the curriculum in the classroom. It focuses on aspects of mindfulness that are most obviously of interest to mainstream educators, including stress, emotion regulation, attention and performance, and then moves on to include work on reflecting on learning, the body and loving kindness.

Scholastic Inc. MindUP : *Brain-Focused Strategies for Learning--And Living.* New York: Scholastic. 2014

There are 3 manuals for this very popular 'MindUP' curriculum, for kindergarten to year 2, years 3 to 5 and years 6 to 8 which has been evaluated and found to be effective in many domains. It combines elements of mindfulness, social and emotional learning and neuroscience at a level appropriate for the students in an attractive and tried and tested format.

Vo, Dzung X. *The Mindful Teen: Powerful Skills to Help You Handle Stress One Moment at a Time.* Oakland: New Harbinger, Instant Help Books, 2015

>This self-help book is written by an experienced paediatrician who works extensively with teens and who has developed his own taught programme based on tried and tested MBSR/MBCT, plus some elements of the work of Thich Nhat Hanh. It talks directly to young people in a simple and practical style, to help them understand and apply practical strategies to deal with stress mindfully, including the pressures of school such as tests and examinations, and improve relationships with family and friends.

Rezek, Cheryl. *Monkey Mind and The Mountain: Mindfulness for 8-80 year olds (and older)*

>Written for children but enjoyed by adults too, this book aims to be a simple and engaging introduction to mindfulness. It recognises our natural ability to be mindful and to use it in a way that can help to both enjoy life and deal with the more difficult aspects of it, such as school pressure, bullying or lack of confidence. Children learn to be accepting to feel a sense of gratitude and to create a reliance on that internal power and belief that can be a guide and compass throughout life. A percentage of profits goes to a charity for vulnerable children.

Rezek, Cheryl. *Monkey Mind and The Mountain: Mindfulness, Mental Health and Resilience for Primary School Children*

>This 42-session programme aims to lay the foundations of good mental health and stability, resilience and resourcefulness, within young children. It aims to teach children about mindfulness, what it is and how to develop it, to learn awareness of themselves both physically and emotionally, and to develop skills on how to manage emotions, difficult times and life experiences. Session times are flexible, it uses animation and cartoons, tasks and adventures, and no training is required. It has been adapted for online use too, allowing for sessions to be sent home when children are unable to attend school. www.lifehappens-mindfulness.com/mindfulness-mental-health-resilience/

APPENDIX 6

References and notes

1. Bishop, S.R., Lau, M., Shapiro, S., Carlson, L., Anderson, N.D., Carmody, J., Segal, Z.V., Abbey, S., Speca, M., Velting, D., and Devins, G. (2004). Mindfulness: A proposed operational definition. Clinical Psychology: Science and Practice, 11(3), 230-241.

2. Crane, R., Brewer, J., Feldman, C., Kabat-Zinn, J., Santorelli, S., Williams, J., & Kuyken, W. (2017) What defines mindfulness-based programs? The warp and the weft. Psychological Medicine, 47(6), 990-999.

3. Killingsworth MA and Gilbert DT. (2010) A wandering mind is an unhappy mind. Science. 330(6006):932. doi:10.1126/science.1192439

4. Baer, R. et al. (2020) Frequency of self-reported unpleasant events and harm in a mindfulness-based program in two general population samples. Mindfulness. Published online December 2020 https://doi.org/10.1007/s12671-020-01547-8

5. Matthieu Ricard argues that the assumption that secular mindfulness practice invariably leads to kindness and compassion may be naïve, and claims these attitudes need cultivating explicitly, for example through what he calls 'caring mindfulness'. See the Huffington Post, April 22. https://www.huffpost.com/entry/caring-mindfulness_b_7118906

6. Gilbert, P. and Chodron (2015) Mindful Compassion: Using the Power of Mindfulness and Compassion to Transform our Lives. Robinson.

7. Bristow, J., Bell, R., Nixon, D. (2020). Mindfulness: developing agency in urgent times. The Mindfulness Initiative. https://www.themindfulnessinitiative.org/agency-in-urgent-times/

8. Layard, R. and Ward, G. (2020) Can We Be Happier? Evidence and Ethics. Pelican Books

9. Vaish, A., Grossman, T. and Woodward, A. (2008). Not all emotions are created equal: The negativity bias in social–emotional development. Psychological Bulletin 134 (3) 383–40. http://www.cbcd.bbk.ac.uk/people/scientificstaff/tobias/Vaish_PsycBull_2008

10. Gilbert, P. (2019) The Compassionate Mind. Robinson.

11. The idea that digital devices are literally addictive, and the psycho-social mechanisms involved is explored at http://sitn.hms.harvard.edu/flash/2018/dopamine-smartphones-battle-time/

12. Gilbert, P. (2019) ibid

13. Can meditation replace detention? See https://zonia.com/can-meditation-replace-detention-surprising-evidence

14. Van Dam, N. T., van Vugt, M. K., Vago, D. R., Schmalzl, L., Saron, C. D., Olendzki, A. and Fox, K. Mind the hype: A critical evaluation and prescriptive agenda for research on mindfulness and meditation. Perspectives on Psychological Science. 13 (1) 36 – 61, 2016.

REFERENCES AND NOTES

15 Purser, R (2019) McMindfulness: How Mindfulness Became the New Capitalist Spirituality. Repeater Books

16 Forbes, D. (2020) Mindfulness and Its Discontents: Education, Self, and Social Transformation. Fernwood.

17 Klingbeil, D .and Renshaw, T. (2018) Mindfulness-based interventions for teachers: A meta-analysis of the emerging evidence base. School Psychology Quarterly. 33 (4), 501–511 http://dx.doi.org/10.1037/spq0000291

18 Khoury, B., Lecomte, T., Fortin, G., et al. (2013) Mindfulness-based therapy: a comprehensive meta-analysis. Clinical Psychological Review. 2013 33(6):763-71.

19 Maynard, B.R., Solis, M.R., Miller, V.L., and Brendel, K. E. (2017) Mindfulness-based Interventions for Improving Cognition, Academic Achievement, Behaviour, and Socio- emotional functioning of Primary and Secondary School Students. Campbell Systematic Reviews:5. DOI: 10.4073/csr2017.5.

20 Dodge, R. et al. (2012) The challenge of defining wellbeing. International Journal of Wellbeing. 2. 10.5502/ijw.v2i3.4.

21 Klingbeil and Renshaw (2018) ibid

22 Hwang, Y., Bartlett, B. Greben, M., and Hand, K. (2017) A systematic review of mindfulness interventions for in-service teachers: A tool to enhance teacher wellbeing and performance. Teaching and Teacher Education. 64, 26-42.

23 Vonderlin, R., Biermann, M. Bohus, M. and Lyssenkm L. (2020) Mindfulness-based programs in the workplace: a meta-analysis of randomized controlled trials. Mindfulness https://doi.org/10.1007/s12671-020-01328-3.

24 Bartlett, L., Martin, A., Neil, A.L., et al. (2019) A systematic review and meta-analysis of workplace mindfulness training randomized controlled trials. Journal of Occupational Health Psychology. 24(1):108-126. doi:10.1037/ocp0000146

25 Baer, R and Kuyken, W. (2016) Is mindfulness safe? https://www.oxfordmindfulness.org/news/is-mindfulness-safe/

26 Baer, R. et al. (2020) ibid.

27 Kabat Zinn, J. (2016) Full Catastrophe Living: Using the Wisdom of Your Body and Mind to Face Stress, Pain, and Illness: 2nd edition. Dell.

28 The impacts of MBSR on health are summarized in Loucks, E.B. Health Effects of Mindfulness-Based Stress Reduction (MBSR): A Review of Systematic Reviews and Meta-Analyses https://www.lclma.org/wp-content/uploads/2020/08/MBSR-Health-Effects-Loucks-3-20-19.pdf

29 Baer, R. (2014) Mindfulness-Based Treatment Approaches: Clinician's Guide to Evidence Base and Applications 2nd Edition. Academic Press.

30 Jennings, P. et al. (2013) Improving classroom learning environments by cultivating awareness and resilience in education (CARE): Results of a randomized controlled trial, School Psychology Quarterly, 28(4): 374-390.

31 Kemeny, M. E. et al. (2012) Contemplative/emotion training reduces negative emotional behavior and promotes prosocial responses. Emotion, 12(2), 338–350

32 Frank, J.L., Jennings, P.A., and Greenberg, M.T. (2016) Validation of the mindfulness in teaching scale. Mindfulness, 7, 155-163.

REFERENCES AND NOTES

33   Hwang et al., ibid (2017)

34   Mental Health Foundation (2020) Teacher Wellbeing Index. https://www.educationsupport.org.uk/resources/research-reports/teacher-wellbeing-index-2020

35   Ofsted (2019) Summary and Recommendations: Teacher Well-being Research Report https://www.gov.uk/government/publications/teacher-well-being-at-work-in-schools-and-further-education-providers/summary-and-recommendations-teacher-well-being-research-report

36   Zarate, K. et al. (2019) Meta-analysis of mindfulness training on teacher well-being. Psychology in Schools 56 (10) 1700-1715.

37   Lomas, T. et al. (2017) The impact of mindfulness on the wellbeing and performance of educators: A systematic review of the empirical literature. Teaching and Teacher Education. 61, 132-141 http://dx.doi.org/10.1016/j.tate.2016.10.008

38   Khoury et al. (2013) (ibid)

39   National Institute for Health and Care Excellence (NICE). Depression in Adults - Recognition and Management: Clinical Guideline. https://www.nice.org.uk/guidance/cg90/resources/depression-in-adults-recognition-and-management-pdf-975742636741

40   Emerson, L-M, Leyland, A, Hudson, K et al. (3 more authors) (2017) Teaching Mindfulness to Teachers: A Systematic Review and Narrative Synthesis. Mindfulness, 8 (5). pp. 1136-1149. ISSN 1868-8527

41   Hwang et al. (2017) ibid

42   Hwang et al. (2017) ibid..

43   Hwang et al. 2017 ibid.

44   Hwang et al. (2017) ibid. p. 39.

45   Public Health England. (2014) The Link Between Health and Wellbeing and Attainment. A Briefing for Head Teachers, School Governors and Teachers. London: Public Health England https://assets.publishing.service.gov.uk/government/uploads/system/uploads/attachment_data/file/370686/HT_briefing_layoutvFINALvii.pdf

46   Black, D. S. (2016) Mindfulness training for children and adolescents: A state-of-the-science review. In K. W. Brown, J. D. Creswell, and R. M. Ryan (Eds.), Handbook of Mindfulness: Theory, Research, and Practice. Guilford.

47   Mental Health Foundation (2020) Mental health statistics: children and young people | Mental Health Foundation

48   Kessler, R.C., Berglund, P., Demler, O., Jin. R., Merikangas, K.R., and Walters, E.E. (2005) Lifetime prevalence and age-of-onset distributions of DSM-IV disorders in the national comorbidity survey replication. Archives of General Psychiatry, 62 (6) pp. 593-602. doi:10.1001/archpsyc.62.6.593.

49   NHS Digital. (2020) Mental Health of Children and Young People in England, 2020: Wave 1 follow up to the 2017 survey Mental Health of Children and Young People in England, 2020:

50   McKeering. P. and Hwang, Y. (2019) A systematic review of mindfulness-based school interventions with early adolescents. Mindfulness 10:593–610 https://doi.org/10.1007/s12671-018-0998-9

51 Durlak, J.A., Weissberg, R.P., Dymnicki, A.B., Taylor, R.D., & Schellinger, K. (2011) The impact of enhancing students' social and emotional learning: A meta-analysis of school-based universal interventions. Child Development, 82, 474– 501.

52 Broderick, P. C., & Metz, S. (2009) Learning to BREATHE: A Pilot Trial of a Mindfulness Curriculum for Adolescents. Advances in School Mental Health Promotion, 2, 35-46.

53 Sibinga E.M, Webb, L., Ghazarian, S.R. et al. (2016) School-based mindfulness instruction: An RCT.' Pediatrics.;137(1): e20152532 (2016).

54 Lantieri, L. Nambiar, M., Harnett, S. and Nacler Kyse, E. (2016) Cultivating inner resilience in educators and students: The Inner Resilience programme. In Schonert-Reichl, Kimberly A. and Roeser, R. W (eds). Handbook of Mindfulness in Education: Integrating Theory and Research Into Practice. New York: Springer. Pp 119-132.

55 Hwang et al., ibid

56 Jennings et al. (2013) ibid.

57 Wigelsworth, M. and Quinn, A. (2020): Mindfulness in schools: an exploration of teachers' perceptions of mindfulness-based interventions, Pastoral Care in Education. 38:4, 293-310, DOI: 10.1080/02643944.2020.1725908

58 Maynard et al. (2017) ibid.

59 Franco Justo, C. (2009) 'Effects of a meditation program on verbal creative levels in a group of students in late secondary education'. Suma Psicológica 16:113–120.

60 Franco Justo, C., Mañas, I., Cangas, A. J., and Gallego, J. (2011) 'Exploring the effects of a mindfulness program for students of secondary school'. International Journal of Knowledge Society Research 2: 14–28. doi: 10.4018/jksr.2011010102

61 Bakosh, L. S., Snow, R. M., Tobias, J. M., Houlihan, J. L., and Barbosa-Leiker, C. (2016) Maximizing mindful learning: mindful awareness intervention improves elementary school students' quarterly grades. Mindfulness, 7 (1), 59–67.

62 Schonert-Reichl, K. A., Oberle, E., Lawlor, M. S., Abbott, D., Thomson, K., Oberlander, T. F. and Diamond, A. (2015) Enhancing cognitive and social–emotional development through a simple-to-administer mindfulness-based school program for elementary school children: A randomized controlled trial. Developmental Psychology, 51(1): 52–66.

63 Dunning. D.L., Griffiths, K., Kuyken, W., Crane, C., Foulkes, L., Parker, J., & Dalgleish, T. (2018) The effects of mindfulness-based interventions on cognition and mental health in children and adolescents - a meta-analysis of randomized controlled trials. Journal of Child Psychology and Psychiatry. 60(3):244-258

64 Schonert-Reichl et al. (2015) ibid.

65 Singh, N. N., Lancioni, G. E., Singh Joy, S. D., Winton, A. S. W., Sabaawi, M., Wahler, R. G., and Singh, J. (2007) Adolescents with conduct disorder can be mindful of their aggressive behaviour. Journal of Emotional and Behavioural Disorders, 15(1): 56–63. http://doi.org/10.1177/10634266070150010601

66 Bögels, S. Hoogstad, B., van Dun, L., Sarah de Schutter, S. and Restifo, K. (2008) Mindfulness training for adolescents with externalizing disorders and their parents. Behavioural and Cognitive Psychotherapy, 36, pp 193-209 doi:10.1017/S1352465808004190

REFERENCES AND NOTES

67 Wellcome Understanding Learning: Education and Neuroscience https://wellcome.org/what-we-do/our-work/understanding-learning-education-and-neuroscience

68 Dorjee, D. (2017) Neuroscience and Psychology of Meditation in Everyday Life: Searching for the Essence of Mind. Routledge.

69 Tang, Y., Hölzel, B. and Posner, M. (2015) The neuroscience of mindfulness meditation. Nature Reviews Neuroscience 16, 213–225 https://doi.org/10.1038/nrn3916

70 Fox, K.C., Nijeboer, S., Dixon, M.L., Floman, J. L., Ellamil, M., Rumak, S.P., Sedlmeier, P. and Christoff, K. (2014) Is meditation associated with altered brain structure? A systematic review and meta-analysis of morphometric neuroimaging in meditation practitioners. Neuroscience and Biobehavioral Reviews. 43:48-73. doi: 10.1016/j.neubiorev.2014.03.016. Epub 2014 Apr 3. PMID: 24705269.

71 Hölzel et al. (2011) ibid.

72 Tang et al. (2017) ibid.

73 Dorjee (2017) ibid.

74 Mak, C., Whittingham, K., Cunnington, R. et al. (2018) Efficacy of mindfulness-based interventions for attention and executive function in children and adolescents—a systematic review. Mindfulness 9, 59–78 https://doi.org/10.1007/s12671-017-0770-6

75 Dunning et al. (2018) ibid

76 Flook, L, Smalley, S.L., Kitil, M.J., Galla, B.M., Kaiser-Greenland, S., Locke, J., Ishijima, E. & Kasari, C., (2010). Effects of mindful awareness practices on executive functions in elementary school children. Journal of Applied School Psychology, 26(1), 70-95.

77 Tercelli, I., and Ferreira, N. (2019) A systematic review of mindfulness based interventions for children and young people with ADHD and their parents. Global Psychiatry, 2, 79 - 96.

78 Tang et al. (2017) ibid

79 Lazar S.W.; Kerr C.E.; Wasserman R.H.; Gray J.R.; Greve D.N.; Treadway M.T.; Fischl B. (2005). Meditation experience is associated with increased cortical thickness. NeuroReport. 16 (17): 1893–1897. doi:10.1097/01.wnr.0000186598.66243.19. PMC 1361002. PMID 16272874.

80 Hölzel B.K.; Ott U.; Gard T.; Hempel H.; Weygandt M.; Morgen K.; Vaitl D. (2008). Investigation of mindfulness meditation practitioners with voxel-based morphometry. Social Cognitive and Affective Neuroscience. 3 (1): 55–61. doi:10.1093/scan/nsm038. PMC 2569815. PMID 19015095.

81 Bernstein, A., Hadash, Y., Lichtash, Y., Tanay, G., Shepherd, K., and Fresco, D.M. (2015) Decentering and related constructs: A critical review and metacognitive processes model. Perspectives in Psychological Science. 10(5):599-617. doi:10.1177/1745691615594577

82 Segal, Z. Williams, M. and Teasdale, J. et al. (2012) Mindfulness-Based Cognitive Therapy for Depression: A New Approach to Preventing Relapse. Second Edition. Guildford.

83 Solem, S., Thunes, S.S., Hjemdal, O. et al. (2015) A metacognitive perspective on mindfulness: An empirical investigation. British Medical Council Psychology 3, 24 https://bmcpsychology.biomedcentral.com/

articles/10.1186/s40359-015-0081-4

84   Neff, K. and McGehee, P. 2010) Self-compassion and psychological resilience among adolescents and young adults. Self and Identity, 9: 3, 225-240.

85   Education Endowment Fund (EFF) Metacognition and Self-regulated Learning Seven recommendations for teaching self-regulated learning & metacognition.Metacognition and Self-regulated Learning | Education Endowment Foundation | EEF

86   Hwang et al. (2017) ibid

87   Flook et al. 2010 ibid

Weijer-Bergsma, E., Formsma, A. R., Bruin, E. I., and Bögels, S. M. (2012). The effectiveness of mindfulness on behavioural problems and attentional functioning in adolescents with ADHD. Journal of Child and Family Studies. 5, 775–787. doi: 10.1007/s10826-011-9531-7

Vickery, C.E. and Dorjee, D. (2016). 'Mindfulness training in primary schools decreases negative affect and increases meta-cognition in children'. Frontiers in Psychology. http://dx.doi.org/10.3389/fpsyg.2015.02025

88   Rosalyn H. Shute (2019) Schools, mindfulness, and metacognition: A view from developmental psychology, International Journal of School & Educational Psychology, 7:sup1, 123-136, DOI: 10.1080/21683603.2018.1435322

89   Tang et al. (2015) ibid

90   Goleman, D. (2020) Emotional Intelligence. 25th Anniversary Edition. Bloomsbury.

91   National Scientific Council on the Developing Child, Harvard University. Excessive Stress Disrupts the Architecture of the Developing Brain. http://developingchild.harvard.edu/wp-content/uploads/2005/05/Stress_Disrupts_Architecture_Developing_Brain-1.pdf

92   Klingbeil et al. (2017) ibid

93   Emerson et al. (2017) ibid

94   Chiesa, A., and Serretti, A. (2010) A systematic review of neurobiological and clinical features of mindfulness meditations. Psychological Medicine. 40(8):1239-52. doi: 10.1017/S0033291709991747

95   Goleman, D. (2020) ibid.

96   Posner, M.I, and Rothbart. M.K. (2009) Toward a physical basis of attention and self-regulation. Physical Life Review. 6:103–120.

97   Vohs and Baumeister (2016) ibid.

98   Emerson et al. (2017) ibid

99   Dunning et al. (2018) ibid.

100   Tang et al. (2015) ibid

101   Fox et al. (2014) ibid

102   Wilde, S., Sonley, A., Crane, C. et al. Mindfulness training in UK secondary schools: a multiple case study

REFERENCES AND NOTES

approach to identification of cornerstones of implementation. Mindfulness 10, 376–389 (2019). https://doi.org/10.1007/s12671-018-0982-4

103   Mendelson et al. (2020) Implementing mindfulness and yoga in urban schools: a community-academic partnership. Journal of Children's Services. 2013;8(4):276–291. doi: 10.1108/JCS-07-2013-0024.

104   Hudson, K.G. Lawton, R., and Hugh-Jones, S. (2020) Factors affecting the implementation of a whole school mindfulness program: a qualitative study using the consolidated framework for implementation research. British Medical Council Health Services Research. 2020;20(1):133

105   Brown, Valerie and Olson, Kirsten (2015) The Mindful School Leader. Sage.

106   Mendelson et al. (2020) ibid

107   Crane et al. (2017) ibid

108   Emerson. L. et al. (2020) Mindfulness interventions in schools: Integrity and feasibility of implementation. International Journal of Behavioral Development. 44(1):62-75. doi:10.1177/0165025419866906

109   Wigelsworth and Quinn, A. (2020) ibid.

110   Mindful Wales (2020) Mindfulness in Wales: a toolkit for introducing mindfulness in education.

111   Beshai, S., McAlpine, L., Weare, K. et al. (2016) A non-randomised feasibility trial assessing the efficacy of a mindfulness-based intervention for teachers to reduce stress and improve well-being. Mindfulness 7, 198–208. https://doi.org/10.1007/s12671-015-0436-1

112   Felver. J. and Singh, N. (2020) Mindfulness in the Classroom: An Evidence-Based Program to Reduce Disruptive Behavior and Increase Academic Engagement. New Harbinger. Based on the 'Soles of the Feet' meditation Broderick, P. (2013) Learning to Breathe, New Harbinger.

113   Crane P, Ganguli P, Ball Ms, et al. (2020) Training school teachers to deliver a mindfulness program: Exploring scalability, acceptability, effectiveness, and cost-effectiveness. Global Advances in Health and Medicine.. Vol 9. doi:10.1177/2164956120964738

114   Durlak, J. (2016) What everyone should know about implementation. In J.Durlak et al. (Eds) Handbook of Social and Emotional Learning Research and Practice. Guildford. 395-405.

115   Emerson. L. et al. (2020) ibid.

116   Meixner T, Irwin A, Wolfe Miscio M, et al. (2019) Delivery of integral mindfulness martial arts in the secondary school setting: Factors that support successful implementation and strategies for navigating implementation challenges. School Mental Health 11(3):549–61

117   Crane et al. (2-17) ibid.

118   Carsley, D., Khoury, B. and Heath, N.L. (2018) Effectiveness of mindfulness interventions for mental health in schools: a comprehensive meta-analysis. Mindfulness 9, 693–707 https://doi.org/10.1007/s12671-017-0839-2

119   Bluestein, J. (2001) Creating Emotionally Safe Schools: A Guide for Educators and Parents. Simon and Schuster

120   See an account of Kolb's experiential learning cycle https://www.simplypsychology.org/learning-kolb.html

121   Huppert, F. A., and Johnson, D. M. (2010) 'A controlled trial of mindfulness training in schools:

REFERENCES AND NOTES

The importance of practice for an impact on well-being' The Journal of Positive Psychology, 5(4): 264–274. http://doi.org/10.1080/17439761003794148

122   Kuyken, W., Weare, K., Ukoumunne, O. C., Vicary, R., Motton, N., Burnett, R., and Huppert, F. (2013). Effectiveness of the mindfulness in schools programme: Non-randomised controlled feasibility study. The British Journal of Psychiatry, 203(2): 126–131.

123   Topping K et al. (2017) Effective Peer Learning: From Principles to Practical Implementation. Routledge

124   Treleaven, D. and Britton, W. (2018) Trauma-Sensitive Mindfulness: Practices for Safe and Transformative Healing. Norton.

125   Burrows, L. (2017) "I feel proud we are moving forward": safeguarding mindfulness for vulnerable student and teacher wellbeing in a community college. The Journal of Adult Protection, Vol. 19 No. 1, pp. 33-46. https://doi.org/10.1108/JAP-08-2016-0015

126   Oritz, R., & Sibinga, M. (2017). The role of mindfulness in reducing the adverse effects of childhood stress and trauma. Children, 4(16), 1-19. https://www.mdpi.com/2227-9067/4/3/16

127   Treleaven and Britton (2018) ibid.

128   Kielty, M., Gilligan, T, and Staton, A.R. (2017) Whole school approaches to incorporating mindfulness-based interventions: Supporting the capacity for optimal functioning in school settings, Childhood Education, 93:2, 128-135, DOI: 10.1080/00094056.2017.1300491

129   Weare, K. (2000) Promoting Mental, Emotional and Social Health: A Whole School Approach. Routledge.

130   Weare, K., & Nind, M. (2011). Mental health promotion and problem prevention in schools: what does the evidence say? Health Promotion International, 26(S1), 29– 69.

131   Public Health England (2015) Promoting Children and Young People's Emotional Health and Wellbeing: A Whole School and College Approach. https://www.gov.uk/government/publications/promoting-children-and-young-peoples-emotional-health-and-wellbeing

132   CASEL (2020) What is SEL? https://casel.org/what-is-sel/

133   Ofsted (2019) Education Inspection Framework. https://www.gov.uk/government/publications/education-inspection-framework/

134   Public Health Wales (2019) Putting health and wellbeing at the core of the new Welsh education curriculum.

135   Lawlor, M. (2016) Mindfulness and social and emotional learning : a conceptual framework. K. Schonert-Reichl, and R. Roeser, (eds). Handbook of Mindfulness in Education: Integrating Theory and Research Into Practice. Springer. 65-82.

136   The Education Endowment Fund (2018) Metacognition and Self-regulated Learning https://educationendowmentfoundation.org.uk/tools/guidance-reports/metacognition-and-self-regulated-learning/

137   Ergas, O. (2018) Reconstructing 'Education' through Mindful Attention: Positioning the Mind at the Center of Curriculum and Pedagogy Palgrave Macmillan.

138   Chaskalson, M. (2011) The Mindful Workplace: Developing Resilient Individuals and Resonant Organizations with MBSR. Wiley-Blackwell.

REFERENCES AND NOTES

139   Sekhon, M., Cartwright, M. and Francis, J.J. (2017) Acceptability of healthcare interventions: an overview of reviews and development of a theoretical framework. British Medical Council (BMC) Health Services Research. 17, 88. https://doi.org/10.1186/s12913-017-2031-8

140   Lewin, K. (1946) Action Research and Minority Problems. Journal of Social Issues. https://spssi.onlinelibrary.wiley.com/doi/abs/10.1111/j.1540-4560.1946.tb02295.x Issue online April 2010.

141   Sagor, R. (2000) Guiding School Improvement with Action Research. Association for Supervision and Curriculum Development. http://www.ascd.org/publications/books/100047/chapters/What-Is-Action-Research%C2%A2.aspx

142   Centre for Evaluation: Process Evaluation. https://www.lshtm.ac.uk/research/centres/centre-evaluation/process-evaluation

143   Some other forms of analysis that are not often used in evaluating exploring mindfulness in education include: narrative analysis, which involves the reformulation of stories presented by respondents, discourse analysis analyses which of naturally occurring talk and all types of written text, grounded theory, where the researcher begins with a set of data, either quantitative or qualitative, then identifies patterns, trends, and relationships among the data, and ethnography, which is the study of a culture, and phenomenological research exploring the lived experience usually of a small number of individuals in depth.

144   https://www.qsrinternational.com/nvivo-qualitative-data-analysis-software/home
https://atlasti.com/

145   The term and concept 'contemplative education' attempts to capture this more inclusive model, and is gaining ground within higher education, and in the US and the rest of Europe: it may be an appropriate model to start to include on work on mindfulness in UK schools.

146   UNESCO (2020) Rethinking Education and Learning. Rethinking education and learning (unesco.org)

147   Bristow, J., Bell, R., Nixon, D. (2020). Mindfulness: developing agency in urgent times. The Mindfulness Initiative. https://www.themindfulnessinitiative.org/agency-in-urgent-times/

www.ingramcontent.com/pod-product-compliance
Lightning Source LLC
Chambersburg PA
CBHW042017090526
44588CB00024B/2887